Steve Hill is a trusted friend of all wh[o]
God, his commitment to Spirit-filled in[.....]
deep passion that eternal souls be reached with [Go]
truth, and power. This book, *Spiritual Avalanche: The Threat of False Teachings That Could Destroy Millions*, is a message deserving our ready welcome as a "word" from the heart of God! I have known Steve for years yet never before felt the pure fire of an urgency such as he conveys now. With such a proven messenger and so decisive a message as delivered here, I especially invite church pastors, elders, and leaders to "hear" this word, and I urge God's people in all places to join me in opening our hearts to a message of solemn warning—as well as high promise, if it is received.

—JACK HAYFORD
CHANCELLOR, THE KING'S UNIVERSITY

Steve Hill's vivid, persuasive, and impassioned evangelistic altar calls helped spark the incredible revival in Pensacola, Florida, that stirred the nation in the 1990s. Now in his book *Spiritual Avalanche* he proves to be as vivid a writer as he is a preacher. His call for repentance and holiness serves as a wake-up call to all pastors and churches to avoid a catastrophic spiritual disaster that could strike at any time.

—VINSON SYNAN
DEAN EMERITUS, REGENT UNIVERSITY

Spiritual Avalanche is a vision God gave to Steve Hill to prevent millions from end-time deception. This heavenly warning will give you the ability to dodge the maze of deception that is flooding the church. This revelation is a gift from God.

—SID ROTH
HOST, *IT'S SUPERNATURAL*

Steve Hill's avalanche vision is a God-ordained message that is greatly needed in this hour. Currently the body of Christ is in a very serious crisis related to diluting the biblical grace message. I urge every believer who seeks to love Jesus with all their heart and who cares about the destiny of the church to read this book, embrace its call, and heed its warning. This is a must-read book.

—MIKE BICKLE
FOUNDER, IHOP-KC

We stood under the fire of God in Brownsville and marveled at the move of repentance and deep works of salvation. My friend Steve Hill, chosen vessel of that revival, has gone almost from death into resurrection, and the flaming pen and tongue are once again calling the nation to tremble and return to the God of our fathers and to a great grace that doesn't coddle the flesh but produces the fire of holiness and jealousy for God. Wake up, America!

—LOU ENGLE
FOUNDER, THECALL

Steve Hill has received a vision from heaven to awaken the body of Christ in this hour. It is a warning from God, a clarion call to us to speak the whole counsel of God's Word and bring correction to what has been misguidance. He urgently warns us all from a heart of love to wake up and save the lives of people who are hanging in the balance of eternity.

—SHARON DAUGHERTY
PASTOR, VICTORY CHRISTIAN CENTER

Steve Hill has never been a people-pleasing preacher. His anointed calls for repentance during the days of the Brownsville Revival provided a strong foundation for that significant move of God. I am grateful that the Lord has raised Steve up to once again to declare the word of the Lord to our generation. With the passing of such prophetic voices as Leonard Ravenhill and David Wilkerson, we need more ministers who will share the cutting truths of God's Word without compromise.

The message contained within *Spiritual Avalanche* will stir you and shake you. Hopefully it will also move you to action.

—BILLY WILSON
EXECUTIVE DIRECTOR, INTERNATIONAL CENTER
FOR SPIRITUAL RENEWAL

This could be one of the most important books of the decade. God has brought Steve Hill back from the jaws of death to bring an urgent warning to the church, and we ignore it to our own peril. The vision is disturbing and compelling, turning us from impending disaster and calling us back to the true gospel.

—MICHAEL L. BROWN, PhD
AUTHOR, NATIONALLY SYNDICATED RADIO SHOW HOST,
AND PRESIDENT, FIRE SCHOOL OF MINISTRY

It takes a trained eye to recognize the threat of an avalanche. It is evident that Steve Hill has seen something and has issued a red alert. God has given Steve a voice to this generation, and he is not afraid to use it to keep us from danger. He also has the heart of God. It is a heart for both saint and sinner. While a strong word flows from his lips, tears flow down from his face. You cannot separate a man from his message.

It is as though God has sovereignly brought Steve back from the jaws of death to once again deliver a solemn warning. Let us hear him!

—JOHN A. KILPATRICK
FOUNDER AND SENIOR PASTOR, CHURCH OF HIS PRESENCE

I met Steve and heard him preach for the first time in 1999. The anointing of the Holy Spirit was dripping from him, with the Lord confirming His Word through salvations, healings, and deliverances. Our hearts bonded that day. Together we are harvesters for and with Jesus Christ and have since ministered side by side in different parts of the world. Steve's sensitivity to the voice of the Holy Spirit is phenomenal, and I believe this book proves it.

—REINHARD BONNKE
EVANGELIST, CHRIST FOR ALL NATIONS

I know Steve Hill as a man of integrity and godly character, one who is powerfully anointed and mightily used. Now God has given a powerful vision to Steve, challenging him to bring the truth of God's Word back into the body of Christ. We are in danger of being "snowed under" by popular preaching that ignores sin, righteousness, and the judgment to come. The Scriptures forewarned what is now being trumpeted in these end times.

—JOHN ARNOTT
CATCH THE FIRE, TORONTO

Steve Hill is one of God's prophetic voices that give a clarion call to the church. This vision will be a catalyst to help bring about the next great awakening that we are all praying for!

—CINDY JACOBS
GENERALS INTERNATIONAL

I have been shaken to my core as I hear and watch the sloppy doctrinal teachings of some leaders today. Steve Hill's experience drops the plumb line of God's Word right in the midst of this apathetic slide and calls our nation and us back to true biblical morality. Grace and truth came by Jesus. To be a disciple of Jesus, you cannot divide Him in half! Take all of Jesus and receive wholeness. I know Steve Hill and his heart for souls and love for truth. Give us more standard bearers in our day!

—James W. Goll
Cofounder, Encounters Network;
director, Prayer Storm; and best-selling author

We live in a critical time—one that will prove to be a defining hour for the body of Christ. The path the church takes today will set the trajectory for future generations. We are the link between the past and the future—the guardians of the sacred truth that has been passed down from our spiritual forefathers who shed their very blood to preserve it. The stakes could not be higher, and in times like these the prophetic voice is especially vital.

Steve's Hill's voice is a trumpet declaring a message of extraordinary urgency. His message will provoke us, it will challenge us, it will disturb us, and it just might spare us—if we will humble ourselves and heed this timely warning. "He who has ears to hear, let him hear what the Spirit says to the church…"

—Daniel Kolenda
Evangelist, Christ for all Nations

Throughout the ages God has sent prophets to deliver advance warnings of impending danger, disaster, or judgment. Usually neither the message nor the messenger was popular. Correction never is. If people heeded the message and truly repented, they received God's grace and mercy instead of judgment. Steve Hill is a modern-day prophet with a timely message from God. In his book *Spiritual Avalanche* the message is clear and profound. An avalanche of judgment is coming, and the choice is ours: judgment or mercy. May God help us to choose mercy. Thank you, Steve, for your boldness to deliver this message.

—David Cerullo
President, Inspiration Ministries

SPIRITUAL
AVALANCHE

SPIRITUAL AVALANCHE

STEVE HILL

CHARISMA
HOUSE

Library of Congress Cataloging-in-Publication Data:
An application to register this book for cataloging has been submitted to
the Library of Congress.
International Standard Book Number: 978-1-62136-532-7
E-book ISBN: 978-1-62136-533-4

13 14 15 16 17 — 9 8 7 6 5 4 3 2
Printed in the United States of America

For the time will come when they will not endure sound doctrine, but according to their own desires, because they have itching ears, they will heap up for themselves teachers; and they will turn their ears away from the truth, and be turned aside to fables.

—2 Timothy 4:3–4

Contents

Dedication

I HUMBLY RECOGNIZE THE WARRIORS WHO HAVE FALLEN PREY to end-time persecution. Their heart cries are literally the unseen foundation for every chapter in this book. One young man who was saved through this ministry wrote, "Pastor Steve, you are my spiritual father, and I will do what you say. However, as a brand-new Christian in a radical Muslim nation, I have a serious decision to make. If I get baptized right now, like the Word commands and you suggest, then my brothers and friends will tie me to a stake and cut off my head."

My response was quite simple and would probably throw many legalistic, biblical law-lovers into a frenzy. I wrote, "I am so proud of your decision to follow Christ. Now, stay on my website and grow in God. It is so important for you to strengthen your relationship with Jesus. In the future God will open doors for you. You will get baptized. Jesus knows it's your desire and will give you wisdom in every step. Right now, rejoice that He loves you and is so proud of your decision to follow Him. Stay in touch, talk to Jesus every day, try to find other believers in your area, but be safe. Love, Steve."

My friend, life is so different outside the Western world. Here we pick up a four-hundred-dollar tennis racket, swing with Olympic strength, and lob the ball across the net. In this young man's country they pick up a four-dollar machete, swing it with terrorist strength, and lob a head into a basket. Many die other horrific ways but *all* for our sweet Jesus. Let's define the number. More than 160,000 baskets are filled every year.[1]

This work is dedicated to martyrs everywhere. They live and die under the guidance of this blessed text: "And they overcame him by the blood of the Lamb and by the word of their testimony, *and they did not love their lives to the death*" (Rev. 12:11, emphasis added).

Most people fear what they might face, or lose, every day. Christian martyrs are different. You probably won't hear their voices, but every drop of their blood screams loud and clear. I just hope that one day I'll have the unprecedented privilege of sitting across from one of them at the marriage supper of the Lamb.

Their blood continues to flow because they refuse to offer another gospel. Western Christians continue to squirm over Scripture. They wrangle and wiggle, hoping to escape the difficult truths in the Word. Who really wins? The battles are so minuscule when laid alongside the bodies of the dead for Christ. We can't seem to die to self while they find it an honor to die for their Savior.

And it is to these true heroes of the faith that this book, based on a vision, is dedicated. For tens of thousands the vision has already drawn the line in the sand. I trust that Jesus will use this truth to radically change the course of the church. If we don't change, we are in for the challenge of a lifetime!

....

NOTES

1. One World Missions, "Missions Education," http://oneworldmissions.com/site.cfm?PageID=5521 (accessed January 28, 2013).

Vision

Vision: A supernatural appearance that conveys a revelation.

> Where there is no vision, the people perish [live without order or direction; they cast off restraint]: but he that keepeth the law, happy is he.
>
> —Proverbs 29:18, kjv

What to do with a vision: Let your vision penetrate you before expecting others to be impacted. Remember, it may be just for your heart only. God will show you. Write it down quickly so others, in time, can benefit from what the Lord is saying. Rely not on memory alone. It will betray you.

> My heart is overflowing with a good theme;
> I recite my composition concerning the King;
> My tongue is the pen of a ready writer.
>
> —Psalm 45:1

> The word of the Lord was precious in those days; there was no open vision.
>
> —1 Samuel 3:1, kjv

The Word of the Lord is precious: An open vision is like a radiant star illuminating a blanket of darkness.

Foreword

PERHAPS YOU KNOW THE NAME STEVE HILL FROM THE noted Brownsville Revival, where he preached hundreds of messages convicting multitudes of their sins and bringing them to the altar of repentance. You may be familiar with his hearing and feeling the hoofbeats of John's pale horse and rider of death, as well as the messages God gave him to bring to the nation during this recent season of near death.

This powerful book, *Spiritual Avalanche*, is birthed from a vision Steve experienced in December 2012. In this vision God revealed to him the condition of the church and what we must do to restore life to dying saints.

I've spent time speaking with Steve about this vision and the need for everyone in the body of Christ today to hear it and take it to heart. We share the same passion and desire for truth.

Everywhere I go, false teachings and heresies seem to have slipped into the church and taken root. Just as Steve has done for many years and is continuing to do, I too remain committed to doing everything possible to stop this flood of fallacies and get Christians back into the true battle. We are at war for souls, and we must not allow anything or anyone to deter us from that assignment.

Steve continues to wave the banner of Christ high. The truth is shouted from the rooftop without apology. It is time for us to take a stand. If we don't, we will be eternally ashamed for our cowardly response in the midst of this godless onslaught that threatens the eternity of millions. Let the challenge from his words lead you to a spiritual change and stoke a new fire from the once-burning embers of your soul!

—PERRY STONE
FOUNDER, VOICE OF EVANGELISM

A Note From the Author

THIS BOOK COMES TO YOU OUTSIDE OF MY NORMAL WRITING style. I have chosen to not fill chapters with quotes and writings of well-known church ancestors, famous evangelists, fathers of the faith, and respected writers of years gone by. This is always a great temptation as I have over four thousand books in my library, many of them hundreds of years old, out of print, and full of incredible stories.

Due to the foundational nature of this book I have felt it best to build on the God-given framework of a vision of an avalanche I recently experienced and to write as He continued to inspire. It is for this reason you will find few references to other writers, alive or deceased, and the omission of a glossary or bibliography at the conclusion.

The only exception that I feel must be included in the prelude of this book is a quote from one of my heroes in the faith. He is a spiritual father to millions and has maintained a life of integrity to billions. I speak of the evangelist Billy Graham, who has always preached the unadulterated gospel and has never wavered from his commitment to the Great Commission. These few words from Brother Graham are being tucked into the beginning for a reason. They serve as a foundational truth that echoes throughout this book.

We in the church have failed to remind this generation that while God is love, He also has the capacity to hate. He hates sin, and He will judge it with the fierceness of His wrath. This generation is schooled in the teaching about an indulgent, soft-hearted God whose judgments are uncertain and who coddles those who break His commandments. This generation finds it difficult to believe that God hates sin.

I tell you that God hates sin just as a father hates a rattlesnake that threatens the safety and life of his child. God loathes evil and diabolic forces that would pull people down to a godless eternity just as a mother hates a venomous spider that is found playing on the soft, warm flesh of her little baby.

It is His love for man, His compassion for the human race, that prompts God to hate sin with such a vengeance. He gave Heaven's finest that we might have the best; and He loathes with a holy abhorrence anything that would hinder our being reconciled to Him.[1]

May God richly bless your reading of *Spiritual Avalanche: The Threat of False Teachings That Could Destroy Millions.*

—STEVE HILL

....

NOTES

1. "Things God Hates" by Billy Graham, September 2001 *Decision Magazine*, © 1955 Billy Graham Evangelistic Association. Used with permission. All rights reserved.

Introduction

T HE RESIDENTS OF PLURS, SWITZERLAND, HAD BEEN ENJOYING a beautiful sunny day. The rainy season had passed; the radiant sunshine was a welcome sight. Spirits were lifted. The afternoon was filled with fun, fellowship, and outdoor family activities. Now, as night approached, everyone was enjoying an evening meal and preparing for a good night's sleep. It would be their last.

What became known as the Rodi avalanche occurred around midnight. It was September 4, 1618. Within seconds the entire village was completely covered in snow and debris. The quaint wooden homes with colorful shutters, the flowerpots that hung in the windows, the one-room schoolhouse, corner market, the town square where local government officials had been discussing the business of the day, the cobblestone streets that just a few hours earlier had been filled with gaiety and laughter, the surrounding pastures with fattened cattle—all the hopes and dreams, now, in a moment, gone!

Yes, the unthinkable occurred without warning. The mountain above gave way. In a moment the entire village was covered, buried, eradicated, wiped off the map. This postcard town, high in the Swiss Alps, became a burial ground, a morgue, for all 1,500 men, women, and children who lived there. Before the deadly avalanche was through, it would claim the lives of 2,427 people. History records that only 4 townspeople escaped the destruction. They were visiting friends in a neighboring village.

The citizens of Plurs were well aware of the dangers of living in the majestic Alps. They knew the avalanche terrains. Fireside stories had been passed down through the years of how avalanches came and where they went. Yes, there were risks, but the joy of living in such a paradise far outweighed the improbable landslide of killer snow. Their standard of living was well above any of their neighbors. They mined the mountains for a mineral called talcum. Their mining techniques often disturbed the stability of the layered snow. Fissures formed in the rocks and strange noises erupted from deep within the mountain where they had mined. The mountain itself seemed to cry out a warning, but the people paid little attention. They were enticed by the riches, warned of the risks, and chose to take the chance.[1]

I can't help but compare our Western mentality with that of these dear Swiss pioneers. They were lured by the wealth of the mountain but at the same time knew they were skating on thin ice. Our society, including the church world, is easily charmed by the promise of prosperity, but we fail to take seriously the consequences of disturbing the God who gave it all.

This book is based on an astounding vision, focusing on a spiritual avalanche that startled my soul. Although it concerns the future, I've chosen to begin by going back into history. When I began to study the worst avalanches on record, this Rodi avalanche jumped out as one of the saddest.

My wife, Jeri, and I have traveled all through Switzerland, stopped in the little villages, stayed with the locals, been mesmerized by the snow-covered mountains, stared for hours at the majestic Matterhorn, and were fascinated by the harmonious cowbells in the valleys. It's a land of enchantment. It's so hard to believe that in the midst of this paradise a disaster occurred that has now affected me hundreds of years later. Even more incredible are the lessons that I'm learning.

Over the years thousands of avalanches have occurred around the world. Many go unnoticed and carry little threat to human life. Back in the 1600s little was known about these killer waves of destruction. Now we know why and where they will most likely occur. Even with this knowledge people still die.

What you are about to read approaches this subject from an entirely different view. This vision, this word from the Lord, places our spiritual lives in the paths of these destructive acts of nature. This revelation has shaken me to my very core. I must warn everyone of the impending danger, and I've begun to do so. The response has been surprisingly positive. It seems that many people want to know if their spiritual lives are in danger. They are hearing a wake-up call and desire to learn more about the warning signs.

I pray that you would take these writings as a personal word from the Lord. This will cause the parallels of today's natural avalanches and the impending deadly spiritual avalanches to come alive and, best of all, become meaningful. We're going to take our time visiting the vision, but more importantly we'll make sure everyone understands the meaning of the message. After all, what good is it if God knocks on your door, wants to have an extremely intimate talk, but you refuse to open it? He wants you to answer, swing the door open, allow Him access, and then sit down and listen.

A quick lesson on how to read this book: Perhaps you've heard it said, "Don't just go through the book, but let the book go through you." As you're reading and something is said that offends or you feel doesn't relate to you, always remember, possibly millions are reading or listening to this visionary book. What may seem irrelevant to you could be shaking the spiritual foundation of someone else. Relax and keep reading. The Lord has something to say to everyone.

For the village of Plurs, Switzerland, it's too late. They didn't have the modern-day warnings and the technology that we do today. Now these warnings of danger are clarion clear. The citizens who choose to live in the Alps today are well aware of the dangers and escape routes.

The question remains, will we spiritually listen and obey? After all, with over nine hundred English translations and paraphrases of the Bible and close to five hundred international translations, do we dare demand more? We should be well aware of the spiritual dangers surrounding us and, hopefully, the escape routes. But what do we do with this knowledge? Of course, you understand by now that you don't have to live in the mountains for this vision to have a strong impact in your life.

An interesting note concerning the killer avalanche of September 4, 1618: one of the only items found in the debris years later were the church bells. I can't help but notice a spiritual significance here. Throughout history church bells have been used to summon the people of the church to come together and also to warn people of impending danger. Perhaps those church bells stand as a symbol of the warning cry that needs to ring out to the church today. Can you hear them ringing? They are asking, "If Christianity continues on the present path, what will remain?"

. . . .

NOTES

1. David Bressan, "The Landslide of Plurs," September 4, 2011, http://blogs.scientificamerican.com/history-of-geology/2011/09/04/september-4-1618-the-landslide-of-plurs/ (accessed January 28, 2013).

Chapter 1

The VISION in LIVING COLOR

THIS IS COMING TO YOU FROM A MAN WHO HAS JUST PASSED through the valley of the shadow of death. I was given just a few days to live. Since my close call with eternity just a short while ago, everything has become clearer. I can hear His whisper. Unabated obedience has become my mandate. That is why I'm writing this word from the Lord.

Before we visit the vision and learn the transforming lessons, I must first lay a fundamental foundation. You see, God wants to speak to all His people. He longs to manifest mysteries. Jesus said, "It has been given to you to know the mysteries of the kingdom of heaven, but to them [the unbelievers] it has not been given" (Matt. 13:11). We all crave to be part of God's inner circle. He has personal words to share with intimate friends, but I'm afraid most of us are too far away.

I learned to listen to God's whisper several years ago while having an intimate conversation with Leonard Ravenhill. Reverend Ravenhill is perhaps best known for his literary classic *Why Revival Tarries.* He was a gifted revivalist and chose to spend several of his

1

last years pouring his heart into hungry evangelists. By the favor of God I was given a place in his life. My wife, Jeri, and I lived just a few short miles from his home. We warmly cherish our many visits with Leonard and Martha, often around a cup of English tea and savoring a plate of fresh, homemade cookies.

One afternoon while sitting in his study, surrounded by thousands of vintage books, Leonard spoke these words to me, "Stevie, come here!" (He could call me anything, as long as he called me.) This request was strange because I was sitting just a few feet away. Regardless, I obeyed and scooted my chair closer. We were now almost touching knees when he again made the request, "Closer, Stevie." My next maneuver had me just a few inches from his face. This was all so strange, but somehow I knew revelation was coming. He then, in a soft tone, asked me to put my ear close to his mouth. When I did, the word came. It was barely audible. In a whisper he said, "Stevie, God has secrets to reveal to you. You must stay close. Very close. He never shouts His secrets."

I am a weeper, and the tears flowed freely. The lesson from this eighty-year-old prophet of God was clear. If I wanted to receive young men's visions (Joel 2:28) and hear His "still small voice" (1 Kings 19:12), then I must stay close. To be "under the shadow" of His wings (Ps. 17:8), I must be intimate. To receive the revelation, I must be leaning on His breast (John 13:23). I backed my chair away from this saint of God, not realizing how impactful those few moments would be.

Are you near enough to receive from Him, or do you need to scoot a little closer? I was whisper close when the Lord gave me this "avalanche" word and warning for the Christian world. Just because He whispered it to me, does that give me permission to write it to you? I don't take lightly this vision from the Lord. Here's a powerful biblical model for all of us:

Now after six days Jesus took Peter, James, and John his brother, led them up on a high mountain by themselves; and He was transfigured before them. His face shone like the sun, and His clothes became as white as the light. And behold, Moses and Elijah appeared to them, talking with Him. Then Peter answered and said to Jesus, "Lord, it is good for us to be here; if You wish, let us make here three tabernacles: one for You, one for Moses, and one for Elijah." While he was still speaking, behold, a bright cloud overshadowed them; and suddenly a voice came out of the cloud, saying, "This is My beloved Son, in whom I am well pleased. Hear Him!" And when the disciples heard it, they fell on their faces and were greatly afraid. But Jesus came and touched them and said, "Arise, and do not be afraid." When they had lifted up their eyes, they saw no one but Jesus only. Now as they came down from the mountain, Jesus commanded them, saying, *"Tell the vision to no one* until the Son of Man is risen from the dead."
—MATTHEW 17:1–9,
EMPHASIS ADDED

What we refer to as "the Transfiguration" Jesus called a "vision." After this incredible display of power He instructed His trusted three to tell no one the vision. That's tough. I can't imagine the inner thoughts of these three as they began to descend. It would seem to be a time for a little boasting, at least to the nine left behind.

DISCERNING WHAT TO SHARE

Many spiritual truths that Jesus shares with us are for our individual eyes and ears only. Other times we are to shout from the housetops: "Whatever I tell you in the dark, speak in the light; and what you hear in the ear, preach on the housetops. And do not fear those who kill the body but cannot kill the soul. But rather fear Him who is able to destroy both soul and body in hell" (Matt. 10:27–28).

Jesus said not to cast our pearls before swine: "Do not give what is holy to the dogs; nor cast your pearls before swine, lest they trample them under their feet, and turn and tear you in pieces" (Matt. 7:6).

Here's the lesson: When God gives you a precious pearl, perhaps one that came out of pain and suffering, be sure and guard your mouth. Not everyone understands or is at that spiritual place to receive. Guard your heart! Guard your tongue. What does a dog know about holiness? A swine or pig has no respect for anything precious.

I've had the filthy job of raising pigs, from slopping them to the slaughterhouse. They eat anything! They would swallow a twenty-thousand-dollar pearl as if it were a piece of chocolate. To a pig nothing has value. Everything is scrap garbage being thrown into their trough.

Now, I'm not calling your friends and neighbors dogs or pigs. I'm simply expounding on the Lord's warning when it comes to intimate truths.

How many times have young Christians received an awesome personal revelation from God, and in their immature excitement they can't wait to tell their unsaved friends or family? The problem? They are about to get blasted from those who don't understand.

> **This vision was not thrown to me; it was placed delicately in my spirit by the Holy Spirit.**

Just because you have reached a level of spiritual maturity doesn't mean that your friends will join in the excitement. Upon receiving

Christ I was cursed by many who were not interested in spiritual things. It was a hard-earned lesson.

Most of what the Lord shares with me is personal and remains in my heart. But I sincerely believe that this avalanche vision is a warning for this hour.

What you are about to read will be received by some and rejected by others.

The following words are precious. This vision was not thrown to me; it was placed delicately in my spirit by the Holy Spirit. There is a brotherhood bond between Jesus and me. He knew that I would receive the word and transfer it with tender hands to teachable hearts. So now we come to the beginning of *Spiritual Avalanche*.

WELCOME TO PARADISE...
WITH A TOUCH OF PERIL

A few days ago, after enjoying quality time with Jesus, I was surprised by an alarming vision. I saw a massive, majestic mountain covered in glistening snow. It reminded me of the Matterhorn in the Swiss Alps. Its peaks were sparkling white, and I was amazed by God's attention to detail. It was so realistic I wanted to go skiing! But I sensed there was more that the Holy Spirit was about to reveal.

As I closed my eyes, the entire mountainside sparkled with lights. I was in a winter wonderland bustling with thousands of vacationers. The ski lodge, condos, hotels, and cabins were at full capacity at this popular resort. The visiting five-star rich, the indebted middle class, and the locals who scrubbed the floors were all part of this picturesque parade. (In our next chapter we'll not only visit the resort but also possibly find ourselves among the crowd.)

I began to discern the details. The excited skiers were not anticipating any danger. And why should they be? They had invested hard-earned money to be at a safe, highly recommended, popular family resort.

The Christian faith is almost identical. Innocent lambs have joined churches, paid their tithes, volunteered, and fellowshipped— all based on a naive trust that the leadership is everything it purports to be. They love the entertainment and enjoy the spoon-fed meals. Meanwhile snow continues to cover the mountain.

I was amazed to be seeing such detail in this vision. But why not? Our God is the master of the meticulous. He paints butterflies, creates billions of unique human beings, makes sure that no two snowflakes are alike, and continually controls the circle of life.

Day quickly turned to night. The skiers, snowboarders, and sports enthusiasts were settling in. Anticipation grew as the snow began to fall. It seemed that everyone headed to bed believing tomorrow would be a day of sheer enjoyment on freshly covered slopes. For an avid skier the exhilaration of being the first one to race down a new blanket of snow is a dream come true.

Throughout the night winter storms dropped several feet of new snow on the slopes. The night ski patrol was put on full alert. Their mission was clear. With the potential of killer avalanches occurring, they quickly took to their posts. Most readers are familiar with the word *avalanche*. By definition it is "a sudden overwhelming appearance and deluge of snow, ice, and mud." It comes from a French word that means "to fall or let down."

I began to weep as the vision, along with its spiritual application, continued to unfold.

The ski patrol operated like a well-trained platoon. Some boarded helicopters manned with small bombs; others jumped on snowmobiles loaded with handheld explosive devices. What seemed to be a strategic group of sharpshooters were stationed at the base, maneuvering anti-tank weapons aimed at the snow-covered peaks. They fired their weapons at strategic points in the avalanche zone to force avalanches before the snow accumulated to a life-threatening depth. Left unchecked, the accumulation of heavy, dense snow packed on top of lighter snow could easily slide down with incredible speed and force, resulting in enormous damage and loss of life.

The Lord began to speak. I trembled.

The fresh, new snow represents false teaching that is steadily falling on the ears of the body of Christ. It has been, and is, a heavy snowfall. The skiers represent believers and nonbelievers trusting the resort for a safe and memorable experience. As Christians we have been warned in Scripture: "Be sober, be vigilant; because your adversary the devil walks about like a roaring lion, seeking whom he may devour" (1 Pet. 5:8). However, several currently popular, awe-inspiring teachings have lulled many into a deep sleep.

Layers upon layers of snow have been steadily covering the solid, traditional truth of Christ. God's Word tells us that foolish teaching in these days will become so fashionable even the most dedicated believer can become deceived. "For false christs and false prophets will rise and show great signs and wonders to deceive, if possible, even the elect" (Matt. 24:24). It's happening before our eyes. One spiritual leader said the other day, "You guys are old-fashioned 'holiness.' We are modern-day 'grace.' You live in bondage, while we can do anything we want."

Pastors and teachers worldwide have succumbed to heretical teachings, including universal reconciliation, deification of man, challenging the validity of the Word of God including His judgments, and even lifting any boundaries, claiming His amazing grace is actually "amazing freedom." You are free to live according to your own desires. Sound familiar? "In those days there was no king in Israel; everyone did what was right in his own eyes" (Judg. 17:6). Many popular, self-proclaimed ministers of the gospel are covering the slopes and will be held accountable for the spiritual death of millions.

Just as the ski patrol did in this vision, those who are aware of what's happening must take swift and accurate action. Their weapons of warfare must be aimed at the peaks and the avalanche terrain to dispel the lies. Apostles, prophets, evangelists, pastors, and teachers must be willing to drop spiritual bombs, fire anti-heresy missiles, and even drive into the danger zones armed with explosive truth to confront this potential avalanche. The spiritual generals of this generation must leave the war room and put their years of experience on the front lines.

> **Satan is "snowing" the saints,
> but it can be stopped.**

Friend, I humbly encourage you to heed this vision and take it before the Lord. This is not just Steve Hill telling a story. I've written it just as it was given, and I've expounded the details in this book under the direction of the Holy Spirit. My responsibility is to share with the body of Christ His words to me. The ears that hear and the hands that obey are out of my control.

Satan is "snowing" the saints, but it can be stopped. In the vision I heard explosions. I saw dedicated Christian soldiers scrambling to do anything it took to bring down this avalanche before devastation occurred.

One of the most powerful weapons we possess to combat this onslaught is the tongue. Let God set yours ablaze by preaching "all the words in red." (I'll explain what I mean by this in chapter 13.) If we take action *now*, the result will be a tearing down of false teaching and a remaining layer of solid, God-given, biblical instruction that will save the lost, heal the sick, and strengthen Christians to do the true work of the ministry.

Now, let's venture into these snow-covered mountains and let the Lord reveal what lies beneath. Truth is the pathway to freedom. When a child tells a lie and then confesses, a heavy weight is lifted from his young spirit. When a child of God believes a lie and then allows Jesus to clarify the truth, a magnificent miracle takes place: "You shall know the truth, and the truth shall make you free" (John 8:32).

Chapter 2

The PERFECT RESORT

A PHONE CALL RECENTLY CAME IN THAT CAUSED MY SPIRIT to rejoice. I knew you deserved to listen in. The person on the line was very reputable. The call was in reference to a large, prestigious church. Though the information was secondhand, I knew the source and was confident the data was accurate. This house of worship had within its acreage everything a church shopper could dream of. The entrance had a foyer that would rival most Western shopping malls.

Later in this chapter you'll read more of the attracting atmosphere of many churches today. And by the way, I have no problem with nice buildings and furnishings. My concerns are extremely deep. They are spiritual. I'm not majoring on minors, and I'm not God's private marshal, running around with a gun cleaning up the town.

Let's get back to the phone call. The voice on the other end said, "The church has just had a message in tongues with the interpretation, and that never happens. It was Sunday morning, the church was packed, and the senior pastor, who actually gave the interpretation, stood up and apologized to the church for drifting from their calling. He said that they were a Pentecostal church and should be accustomed to what they'd just heard. Then he did something that shocked the majority of the parishioners. He said, 'We are returning to our roots. How many here today want to be a Pentecostal church? Raise your hands if you're with me!'"

The voice on the line said, "Out of thousands, over a *third* refused to back their pastor. They wanted an easygoing, non-offensive garden for guests. They were rejecting the fire of God, His power, and Holy Ghost tongues. That, in their carnal minds, should all be relegated to a back room or the home fellowship groups!"

If you're reading this and do not have a Pentecostal heritage, keep going. This is about fundamental truth, not nit-picking theological issues that have embattled the church for centuries.

> **If what we are teaching and preaching from our pulpits today is actually a fresh word from God, then why is this nation falling into such disrepair?**

My reaction to this caller's story was, "Wow! The sword came down. How awesome!" If that surprises you, let me say it is never my intention to degrade, destroy, or dismantle anything the Lord has done or is doing. However, we must be blatantly honest in order to move forward in our personal and corporate walk with the Lord.

My spirit has been saturated with concern over the condition of the church. I've asked myself this question many times: If what we are teaching and preaching from our pulpits today is actually a fresh word from God, then why is this nation falling into such disrepair? We are moving away from righteousness and deeper into ungodliness.

I am reminded of Nehemiah's plummeting, personal spiritual condition after hearing of the state of affairs in Jerusalem: "The survivors who are left from the captivity in the province are there in great distress and reproach. The wall of Jerusalem is also broken down, and its gates are burned with fire" (Neh. 1:3). It wasn't good news. Nehemiah wept, fasted, prayed, repented both corporately and personally, and then did what he could to change the dilemma.

I am following in Nehemiah's footsteps. This vision has been received by a broken man. I thank God for His nearness: "The LORD is near to those who have a broken heart, and saves such as have a contrite spirit" (Ps. 34:18). The truth behind this revelation has been producing a steady flow of salty tears. It seems every time I share it, the tear ducts open up. It's uncontrollable. I know heaven is weeping and understands the pain: "'Now, therefore,' says the LORD, 'turn to Me with all your heart, with fasting, with weeping, and with mourning'" (Joel 2:12).

Heaven is concerned over the spiritual condition of His people. One misinformed pastor recently said that God is happy and filled with joy over today's church. His exact words were, "God is glad!" His myopic spiritual insight is not only wrong but also injurious to the flock.

Allow me to share a story that I feel gives a better illustration of where we truly are. The other day I was in a men's store purchasing a shirt. My phone rang and I answered. It was a pastor who wanted to talk about the avalanche vision. Within moments I was sobbing in front of two dozen curious customers. This might not seem too surprising, but what happened next was profound. The assistant manager saw me, came up, somehow knew who I was, and began repenting of his sins. This type of emotional drama occurs quite often. It's all amazingly connected to the vision.

What does this show us? My friend, God is not giving us more time to party. He's giving us space to repent! Have you ever read the passage, "I gave her time to repent of her sexual immorality, and she did not repent" (Rev. 2:21)? We serve an amazingly patient God, but He has His limitations.

Like Nehemiah I have asked God to forgive us and to wash me from anything that brings Him shame. Now, it's time to do something about it.

> **God is not giving us more time to party.**
> **He's giving us space to repent!**

WELCOME TO WESTERN CHRISTIANITY TODAY

Here we go! Let's take a look at the remarkable resemblance of the vacation resort and today's Western churches, small, medium, and large. As I share some of these truths, please don't get angry, slam the book closed, or turn off your electronic edition. I am merely sharing what I saw and what I see. And may I add, if you are in relationship with Jesus, you too can hear from Him. He wants to speak to you. "My sheep hear My voice, and I know them, and they follow Me" (John 10:27).

The vacation resort in the vision is inviting to everyone. If you haven't visited one of these picturesque paradises, then please allow me to paint the picture. My wife and I are familiar with many such places. Jeri and I, along with our three grown children, are snow skiers. Although we haven't had the thrill of skiing the Canadian mountains or the Alps, we have experienced the exhilaration of flying down the slopes of the Rockies, the Appalachians, mountains in the Northeast, and the Andes of South America.

We have found that most resorts are alike, and even most

mountains have similar twists and turns. We are good skiers, not great. We are definitely not heli-skiers (dropped from helicopters). The ultimate goal for us is to enjoy getting to the bottom with no broken bones and, of course, standing up.

For all you snowboarders, I envy your skill and flawless, fearless feats. But you scare me. I enjoy it when you blur by on the slopes, and I hope you will always give us space to slide by. Our occasional crashes have not been that severe. Not yet.

My personal understanding of the sport along with the incredible similarities of ministry, its perils, and responsibilities may be one of the reasons God downloaded this vision into my spirit. But you don't have to be as familiar with skiing as I am to grasp the impact of what I'm about to describe. The correlation between the vision and the modern-day church is striking, down to the last detail.

So let's continue. As I said, the scene was inviting. Everything was perfect at the resort. The last thing you want to experience upon arriving at a ski village is just a dusting of snow and warming temperatures. This was the opposite. It was beyond beautiful.

Every detail was being revealed in seconds. I saw a snow-covered village in living color, international restaurants, and an endless array of stores. If you wanted it, they had it. If you didn't want it, they'd try to sell it to you. In the vision I was living everything in fast motion. Every detail appeared quickly, clearly, and—what is more amazing—unforgettably. There were ski shops pushing the latest gear, even to those who had no intention of getting on the slopes.

How many Christians have purchased materials such as CDs, DVD sermon series, books, magazines, or T-shirts, all because they were caught up in the moment? Like the ski shopper they had no intention of filling up their card with more spiritual products.

Many of these items have never been opened. They adorn shelves, attract dust, and worst of all, drastically drain our bank accounts.

By the way, I have a ski outfit from Norway that I "couldn't live without." The salesman helped convince me that my physique would be transformed in this slick, black one-piece wonder. I would look like a speed racer on the slopes. It would help me tackle double-diamond runs due to its streamlined design and perfect fit. I bought it. Wore it twice. Let's drop the subject.

There was the aroma from open-air coffee stands, hot chocolate kiosks specializing in fresh caramel-stuffed churros, and, of course, jingle-bell-horse-drawn sleigh rides. Everything for everybody.

As a church, how attractive do we have to be? As saints search for the perfect church, today's pastor is under tremendous pressure to cater more and more to picky parishioners. Facing declining attendance and a dwindling bank account, the spiritual leader comes to the conclusion that "much prayer" is not the only answer to his woes. If he is going to be successful, he must look to others who have found the success that has eluded him.

He signs up for the latest conference put on by a local megachurch in hopes of learning the techniques that are guaranteed to work. He attends as many workshops and sessions as he can, taking careful note of everything. It doesn't take long for this pastor to realize that the teachings center more on sound business practices rather than on spiritual, biblical principles.

Of course everything is packaged with just the right amount of religious talk to give the pretense of being spiritual, but the core of the teaching is born in the soul. Deep in his spirit the man of God senses something is off but quickly rationalizes it away, believing that the end justifies the means. He tells himself, "We will reach more people, win more souls, and do more for the community."

Valid desires, no doubt. The temptation has reached a feverish pitch. Now he will finish in the flesh what started in the spirit.

At this precise moment the snow begins to fall. It doesn't take long for the next layer, and the next, and the next. They pile up. This is the precursor of a devastating avalanche.

The pastor comes home and immediately gets to work implementing the new programs and philosophies he has acquired. It's as easy as one, two, three. Set the atmosphere, provide ample amenities, and adjust the message. (One of the teachings at a local conference was to *never* let the Sunday morning crowd know what you believe. Let me paraphrase: Just let it snow; make sure they enjoy themselves so they'll come back.)

Let's complete our picture of the modern-day church. The pastor and his associates waste no time getting to work on creating a proper atmosphere. Guests must be welcomed to a warm and friendly environment that sets them at ease. Religious items must go so that "seekers" are not immediately turned off to offensive images. A portrait of Jesus on the cross and another of Jesus washing the disciples' feet are taken down and replaced with abstract art. Counters that once showcased missions and evangelism are thrown out to make room for bistro tables. A few coats of paint, new furnishings, and soon the entrance to the church rivals the local coffeehouse. Members are ecstatic as they can now fill up on tasty pastries and sip cappuccinos from the comfort of an easy chair before, during, and after service.

Ahh! The perfect resort.

The foyer was just the first step in setting the right atmosphere. The worship team is now coached to the next level. The service is rehearsed several times to nail down every second so as not to waste a moment. The worship experience might kick off with a secular song right off the pop charts. (Yes, this does happen.) This brings the congregation together and sets the tone for the service.

The next two songs are fully rocked-out versions from the latest worship album, complete with high-energy lighting and just the right amount of fog. The set completes with a touching yet worshipful melody that calms even the most hardened of hearts. Skillfully the worship leader brings the audience into a moment of prayer with their eyes closed and hands uplifted. It creates a moment for the stage to be cleared and fully reset for the message. It's a perfectly executed experience that tickles the soul yet fails to touch the spirit. The feedback is immediate and positive. The congregation loves the "worship" the church provides.

With the atmosphere set, the pastor moves on to step two: ample amenities. It's important that a church is a one-stop shop. The kids' program has to be top-notch, featuring the latest gadgetry. It's of vital importance that the children beg their moms and dads to bring them back next week. The church spends tens of thousands of dollars creating a space that would fit in at any theme park. The program is creative, engaging, and definitely kid friendly.

The youth group gets an overhaul as well. A space is cleared out for a game room filled with flat screens, entertainment consoles, pool tables, and cafe. The weekly program is adjusted to allow more time for fellowship and less for a message.

The adults are not left out either. There is something for everyone. The church starts to offer classes for everything from weight loss to self-defense. Nearly every interest in the church is covered through a specialized life group. The atmosphere of community is fostered, and the church immediately begins to grow.

Finally the pastor moves to the final part of the plan: adjusting the message to fit a culturally diverse and increasingly politically correct congregation. The pastor no longer delivers sermons; he brings a "talk." These "talks" are relevant messages lifted out of movies or cultural trends and center on the pleasant themes of the New Testament, such as love, hope, grace, blessing, and forgiveness. Other subjects that might cause listeners to tune out, such as sin, repentance, and judgment, are rarely, if ever, fully touched. Each message is well prepared, properly illustrated, and done in under the clock.

Not all of these things are bad. Many are tools that we have used in the past to reach people. The danger is found in the fact that *it is possible to grow a church completely with these tools.* There is no need for God to build the house when we have it down to a predictable, calculated science.

GOD'S IDEA OF THE PERFECT CHURCH

I once sat down with a pastor who walked me through the first two years of a church plant. The equation figured everything down to the penny. He gloated over the fact that he could plant a church anywhere. I was grieved because not once did he mention prayer, fasting, or even a burden for the city. It was simply another store in the perfect church franchise.

> **We've created an atmosphere where man feels accepted but God feels rejected.**

"I am afraid that I can do all of this without any help from God," I penned in my journal decades ago. I knew that with talent, a little treasure, and the right timing I could pull off church planting without God. Frightening words.

The church has worked hard to make itself attractive to the flesh at the expense of becoming appalling to God. We've created an atmosphere where man feels accepted but God feels rejected. The other day a friend read me a flier that was neatly hung on his doorknob. He cracked up and knew I would too. It was called the "No Church," and I quote: "Tired of church? Come to the No Church. No choir, no congregational singing, no sermon, no offering, and no altar call. If you're tired of church, come join us. The No Church might be what you're looking for. We're here for you!" No kidding!

I assure you, God's idea of the perfect church looks drastically different from ours. I've spent some time on this subject in this chapter not to create negative feelings, but to emphasize where God was taking me in the vision.

The Lord was giving me an immediate parallel interpretation for many of the events taking place: most churches, just like resorts, cater to the crowd. Of course resorts will do anything and everything to attract the money to maintain the machine. That's their materialistic business. I don't want to go to a resort of any kind that doesn't cater to me. I'm paying hard-earned money. I want attention! They offer lift ticket specials, buy-three-nights-get-the-fourth-free hotel values, discount ski rentals—the list is endless. That's the world. The church, on the other hand, should never cater to the crowd's desires; they should *change* the crowd's desires.

Calvary wasn't comfortable. The cross was a painful torture. We are to be crucified with Him, as Paul said, "I have been crucified with Christ; it is no longer I who live, but Christ lives in me; and the life which I now live in the flesh I live by faith in the Son of God, who loved me and gave Himself for me" (Gal. 2:20).

Remember, Christ ran the crowd off. He knew they needed a *message*, not a *massage*. Let's go back a couple thousand years. Jesus said to them, "Most assuredly, I say to you, unless you eat the flesh of the Son of Man and drink His blood, you have no life in you. Whoever eats My flesh and drinks My blood has eternal life, and I will raise him up at the last day. For My flesh is food indeed, and My blood is drink indeed. He who eats My flesh and drinks My blood abides in Me, and I in him" (John 6:53–56).

> **The church should never cater to the crowd's desires; they should *change* the crowd's desires.**

I'll give you a synopsis of the rest of His discourse. Jesus was teaching in the synagogue. The crowd of disciples didn't like the teaching. They wanted sweets; He was serving veggies. So they got up and left. Pastor, when was the last time anyone got up and left? You're not running a country club; you're supposed to be pastoring crucified Christians.

Jesus was not in the catering business. He refused to give them what they wanted. He was under a mandate from God to give them what they needed. Have you ever noticed that many of His disciples turned away from Him, never to return?

> From that time many of His disciples went back and walked with Him no more. Then Jesus said to the twelve, "Do you also want to go away?" But Simon Peter answered Him, "Lord, to whom shall we go? You have the words of eternal life. Also we have come to believe and know that You are the Christ, the Son of the living God."
>
> —John 6:66–69

This should speak volumes to those who find themselves constantly being *stroked* by preaching but never receiving a *strike*. When was the last time you got a good spanking in church?

COVERING SIN WITHOUT REMOVING IT

Let's get back to the snowy scene at the resort. Have you ever noticed how fresh fallen snow covers everything? Even the dirtiest parts of town look inviting due to the white icing. Your backyard could be dull and dead, but after a good snowfall it's sparkling white. It's also remarkable how a steady flow of pleasant teaching can cover sin without removing it.

What a scene! A social mecca! Everything you need and don't need is at this glistening recreation center. It's the church, ready to satisfy man's cravings for God's goodness and goodies. Today's Western church has all the attractions of an amusement park. It's a five-star resort, but I'm afraid it will receive a bad report, according to Scripture. There is a text in the Word of God that I'm afraid reflects our present day, people-pleasing, perfect resort:

> And to the angel of the church of the Laodiceans write, "These things says the Amen, the Faithful and True Witness, the Beginning of the creation of God: 'I know your works, that you are neither cold nor hot. I could wish you were cold or hot. So then, because you are lukewarm, and neither cold nor hot, I will vomit you out of My mouth. Because you say, "I am rich, have become wealthy, and have need of nothing"—and do not know that you are wretched, miserable, poor, blind, and naked—I counsel you to buy from Me gold refined in the fire, that you may be rich; and white garments, that you may be clothed, that the shame of your nakedness may not be revealed; and anoint your eyes with eye salve, that you may see. As many as I love, I rebuke and chasten. Therefore be zealous and repent. Behold, I stand at the door and knock. If anyone hears My voice and opens the door, I will come in to him and dine with him, and he with Me. To him who overcomes I will

grant to sit with Me on My throne, as I also overcame and sat down with My Father on His throne. He who has an ear, let him hear what the Spirit says to the churches.'"

—REVELATION 3:14–22

Now let's move on to discuss what happens when the church focuses on pleasing men instead of pleasing God.

Chapter 3

COME ONE, COME ALL

I F YOU'VE EVER BEEN TO A WINTER RESORT, YOU KNOW THAT they attract every type of snow sports enthusiast. The atmosphere has an international flavor to it. People come from all over the world and from all walks of life. The resort in my vision was no different. It was bustling with crowds of people and welcoming to all. And the spiritual parallel is too wonderful to pass up. Just as the resort attracts everyone, Jesus attracts everyone! He said, "I, if I am lifted up from the earth, will draw *all* peoples to Myself" (John 12:32, emphasis added). What a Savior!

As an evangelist I've had the privilege of preaching to millions, from the extremely rich to the most humble poor. I am convinced that when Jesus, the cross, His sacrifice, and the healing power of His blood are proclaimed, the good news draws the crowd. Not only does the cross of Christ draw all people, but it also transforms anyone who is ready and willing. I have seen hundreds of thousands literally run for their lives to the altar. It never grows old. The next night many of the new converts are back with their friends, hoping that they too will be drawn to Jesus.

Jesus draws everyone to Himself, but what does He say? "Follow Me. Take up your cross. There's a cost involved. This life will change you." Becoming His follower isn't something you *add* to your identity; it *redefines* your identity. If the cross of Christ is truly preached, it is transforming.

In the vision the resort was welcoming to everyone, but there were rules. There were procedures designed to keep people as safe as possible. There were training sessions for beginners. You can't ski down a double-black diamond until you've first mastered the bunny slope. Everyone is welcome, but training and growth— transformation—must happen.

The church should be the same. People's lives should change as they are brought to repentance for their sins. Biblical principles and standards should be followed without compromise, regardless of ministry position or social standing.

But sadly this is not the case in most of our churches today. Instead of the true gospel, people are fed a lukewarm, pitiful, watered-down message of the cross of Christ, adding more layers of accumulating snow up on the mountain. More layers are added as more liars are given platforms.

Yet it's not totally the fault of the preacher or televangelist. People are craving something different to eat, something easier to swallow. "Don't you have a message that will get me to heaven without all the pain and sacrifice?"

They jump on the heretical bandwagon without realizing it. Why? They're tired of the old. They don't want their dad's religion. They don't want the God of their grandma or, for that matter, the God of Moses or Noah. They don't want those kiddie stories; they want something that is current for today. They think none of that old religion relates. (You will enjoy more of this truth in chapter 14.)

Ironically this problem of people wanting something new is anything *but* new. Isaiah dealt with it over twenty-five hundred years ago. Read it for yourself. If you don't like the New King James

Version, that's cool. Pick a translation, not a paraphrase, and follow along:

> Now go, write it before them on a tablet,
> And note it on a scroll,
> That it may be for time to come,
> Forever and ever:
> That this is a rebellious people,
> Lying children,
> Children who will not hear the law of the LORD;
> Who say to the seers, "Do not see,"
> And to the prophets, "Do not prophesy to us right things;
> Speak to us smooth things, prophesy deceits.
> Get out of the way,
> Turn aside from the path,
> Cause the Holy One of Israel
> To cease from before us."
>
> —ISAIAH 30:8–11

Can you believe that? Centuries ago people wanted their own way. They wanted the easy way out. They wanted to hear something new and different. They were looking for a change, even if it was a lie.

GETTING AN ACCURATE WEATHER REPORT

In many ways prophets are like weather reporters. They hear from God and broadcast what He is saying. In the vision radio DJs and TV reporters were screaming out the good news. They were giving a weather report that is exactly what everyone wanted to hear: "The weather is changing! Snow is coming!" And the people were flocking to the resort.

This is exactly what happens in a real ski resort. During the ski season the snow enthusiasts are glued to the meteorological reports.

If the news is good, they grab their gear, vacate their premises, and head to the mountains.

Now, if you were going skiing, would you want the truth about the weather or take your chances? Do you want a made-up weather report to make you feel good about skiing or the facts that will allow you to decide?

> **Believers should be embarrassed with themselves for wanting something more than the cross. It's all been covered on Calvary.**

Sadly, many people in our churches today are happy to listen to inaccurate reports. "Please, someone, bring me some different news! Give my tired, itchy ears something to feel good about! Don't talk about sin and hell! Just talk about God's blessings." I call these "shouts of shame."

Believers should be embarrassed with themselves for wanting something more than the cross. It's all been covered on Calvary. Your cup in life is crucifixion. What more do you need than what's already been done?

Paul made it plain to the church in Corinth when he wrote:

> I, brethren, when I came to you, did not come with excellence of speech or of wisdom declaring to you the testimony of God. For I determined not to know anything among you except Jesus Christ and Him crucified. I was with you in weakness, in fear, and in much trembling. And my speech and my preaching were not with persuasive words of human wisdom, but in demonstration of the Spirit and of power, that your

faith should not be in the wisdom of men but in the power of God.

—1 CORINTHIANS 2:1–5

My friend, there's nothing more God can do, and there is nothing more you need!

When people keep mandating to hear a new word from God, leaders can cave under the pressure and embellish, sugarcoat, or completely fabricate a "weather forecast" in order to meet the demand. This is when they start operating in the flesh and get into error.

It reminds me of the people in Jeremiah's time. Jeremiah, who was called the weeping prophet, heard these words from God:

> The prophets prophesy lies in My name. I have not sent them, commanded them, nor spoken to them; they prophesy to you a false vision, divination, a worthless thing, and the deceit of their heart. Therefore thus says the LORD concerning the prophets who prophesy in My name, whom I did not send, and who say, "Sword and famine shall not be in this land"— "By sword and famine those prophets shall be consumed!"
>
> —JEREMIAH 14:14–15

Let me establish a truth right now. Modern-day prophets exist and are operating all over the world. Many of my friends hear directly from God, and they pray, weep, agonize, travail, and oftentimes wait before proclaiming, "Thus saith the Lord." They can be scary if you're living in sin. They're friends if you're in fellowship with Jesus. They'll stand before God and be held accountable, just like you and me, if they're operating in the flesh.

Prophets need to foresee the storm, use godly wisdom to identify the layers of heresy, and warn the church. Some do, but many fear the fallout of speaking truth. David Wilkerson called them "pillow prophets." Instead of warning, they proclaim, "Everything is wonderful, grab your skis, hit the slopes!" It doesn't bring in the dough when they predict bad snow.

I hurt for the hearers and mourn for the messengers. They poison the people. They inject killer viruses into the body of Christ. Without any remorse or the fact that they may be totally wrong, they march on with their medicines. Those who were spiritually healthy become sick. Where is the brokenness? God says, "Talk no more so very proudly; let no arrogance come from your mouth, for the LORD is the God of knowledge; and by Him actions are weighed" (1 Sam. 2:3).

WE'VE TURNED AWAY FROM THE TRUTH

Someone called while I was writing this chapter. I normally turn my phone off and write in a quiet place, but today was different. Their call, from another country, was desperate: "What's going on, Brother Steve? I've never seen or heard such heresy. It's sweeping all over the world. We must do something. This teaching is blinding the eyes of those who want to believe. They want to repent but are being told that it's not necessary. Jesus has already taken care of it. They are remorseful, broken, and want to pour out their sins, but they're being instructed that repentance of that nature is no longer God's desire."

My friend, could you imagine if John the Baptist had entered the scene with that kind of religious jargon? It's impossible to see that prophet of God soft-peddling the coming of the Chosen One. His pronouncement was clear: "Behold! The Lamb of God who takes away the sin of the world" (John 1:29).

In the days of John the Baptist the people were desperately ready for a spiritual climate change. They heard through the grapevine that a different kind of religious man was trumpeting some incredible news. He was even speaking of someone else coming, someone who had even more clout and connection with God than he did.

> **I think pastors need to repent for not challenging people to repent.**

In those days the news of the Lord's appearing caused waves of religious wanderers to come and listen to His forerunner. This story, with the exclusion of my brief commentaries, can be found in Matthew 3: "In those days John the Baptist came preaching in the wilderness of Judea, and saying, 'Repent, for the kingdom of heaven is at hand!'" (vv. 1–2).

Repent is a word rarely heard inside the walls of the church. By definition it is very offensive. To repent you *must* admit that you are wrong and humbly change positions. Actually, you turn around and go the other way. Most modern-day parishioners don't want to hear that "old-fashioned" message and often vocalize their opinion. What's even sadder is that most pastors today pay more attention to what the people *want* than what they *need*. I think pastors need to repent for not challenging people to repent.

John continued:

> For this is He who was spoken of by the prophet Isaiah, saying: "The voice of one crying in the wilderness: 'Prepare the way of the LORD; make His paths straight.'" And John himself was clothed in camel's hair, with a leather belt around his waist; and his food was locusts and wild honey. Then Jerusalem, *all*

Judea, and *all* the region around the Jordan went out to him
and were baptized by him in the Jordan, confessing their sins.
—Matthew 3:3–6,
emphasis added

Please bear with me as I emphasize the word *all*. It seems small
and insignificant, but on the contrary, it carries incredible spiritual
power. The original Greek meaning of the word *all* in this passage
means "all, everyone, no exclusions."

So to paraphrase, this scripture about John the Baptist was
saying, "And then *all, everyone, no exclusions* came out to hear the
maniacally dressed messenger." His words pierced the walls of religious rhetoric. The common folks loved it. He made sense!

The word *all* is just as universally inclusive as the word *whoever*
or *whosoever*: "And it shall come to pass that *whoever* calls on the
name of the Lord shall be saved" (Acts 2:21, emphasis added). "For
God so loved the world that He gave His only begotten Son, that
whoever believes in Him should not perish but have everlasting life"
(John 3:16, emphasis added). What an advertising campaign for
Jesus! And I've just touched the surface.

Oh, did I fail to mention that John 3:16 is a judgment scripture as
well as a love scripture? Read it again, or just recite it from memory.
Doesn't it say that we were all *perishing*? I think Jesus was referring to hell in His conversation with Nicodemus, don't you? I don't
think He was saying that we were all perishing to paradise or that
we were going to all perish in a baptismal pool. (I'll discuss this
further in chapter 13.)

Can you see the analogy? John the Baptist screamed above the
crowds and drew them to the good news just like the weather
reporters in the vision. Only he didn't make it up; he didn't sugarcoat it or tickle their ears. He preached the truth. He pointed to

Jesus. And the people left their comfort zones to join this man who had a radical message for everyone.

STOP MAKING YOUR OWN SNOW

Since the foundation of time it's all been recorded. God is omniscient: "Great is our LORD, and mighty in power; His understanding is infinite" (Ps. 147:5). He knew that the time would come when men and women would grow tired of the same old stuff.

You'll see the following text several times throughout this book. I want the Spirit of God to cement this passage to your heart:

> For the time will come when they will not endure sound doctrine, but according to their own desires, because they have itching ears, they will heap up for themselves teachers; and they will turn their ears away from the truth, and be turned aside to fables.
>
> —2 TIMOTHY 4:3–4

I believe that most people reading this book have a basic understanding of the Bible. This previous scripture means that believers will no longer be satisfied with just the traditional teachings of the Word. After all, it's a new day. Why not deliver some new teaching that fits into today's freewheeling society? They say, "Give me something for my lifestyle. If you don't, I'll find someone who will. I'm tired of waiting."

Well, so were the people of God in the time before Jesus was born. Between Malachi and Matthew there were many silent years. The spiritual ground was dry; the children of Israel were thirsty. There had been no fresh word from God for generations.

Imagine what it's like to be at a resort in the middle of snow country bankruptcy, a season of drought. The resort depends on several months of snow and cold climate, and if snow doesn't fall from above, then the artificial machines will make it. But if the temperature is not around freezing, there will be no snow, no skiers, no snow making, and, of course, no bustling resort. No money.

When the spiritual climate is not suitable to modern believers, then why not make some changes? Let's offer up something different. Let's make our own snow. Let's manufacture a word from God. My friend, this is frightening. You are setting a deathtrap for millions. Remember, you don't live alone on Planet Earth. We are all connected, and unfortunately we influence one another without even knowing.

Once you start making your own snow, anything goes. Yes, houses of worship across our nation are buzzing with activity: "Tell your neighbor. Everyone is saved. There are no judgments. You have to hear our pastor. He's amazing!"

One minister invited his church to go door-to-door with a loaf of bread and a bottle of wine. "Give them as a token of our church's love. Come one, come all!"

Another sad situation is a church I know of that encourages BYOB (bring your own booze) parties, sanctioned by the church, to be held at private homes so as not to offend any new outsiders.

There are pulpits where the word *sin* is never permitted to be spoken.

Come one. Come all. Fresh snow is falling.

In the vision, at the announcement of fresh snowfall everything else was canceled. People came from everywhere and blended into the exciting culture. Snowboarding, sledding, ice skating, tubing, and, of course, skiing—from bunny slopes to double-black diamonds—were all part of the attractions.

You don't even have to be a snow enthusiast to enjoy a resort like this. You can hate snow but still come. The scenery is worth it all.

It's hauntingly similar to what I heard one man say about a large, resort-like church: "I don't believe like they do, but the music is sure good."

It could be the brilliant light show, entertaining musicians, a bouncy-ball children's program, fellowship around a hot cup of latte, or more. The Western church has campaigns and programs that appeal to every spiritual level of believer. "Come one, come all. Even if you're from another religious persuasion, welcome! We won't offend you. You can stick with your religious beliefs, serve your god, and still come here. Everyone is welcome, and everyone is going to heaven."

You better be ready if you come to a church where I'm preaching because I will welcome you with open arms, but then you're going to hear the truth. For starters, the truth is there's only *one* way to heaven and nobody gets special treatment based on the size of their bank account, their title, or their social status.

It's time to quit changing the forecast to tell people what they want to hear. It's time to stop making our own snow. It's time to stop giving people what they want and start giving them what they need.

> **I often wonder how many of today's peace, love, and freewheeling grace preachers would quickly change their message if the money dried up.**

A man came up to me on a recent Sunday after church. He shook my hand and thanked me, saying, "I love this church. Thank you so much for telling the truth. I was at another church for years, and nobody ever confronted me once about my sin. I had been living with my girlfriend for years. Thank you for caring enough about my soul to confront me about my sin."

Yes, the church is for everybody. All are welcome. Jesus came to seek and save the lost. And certainly it's a place for people to have the freedom to grow and mature in Christ, and that is a process. But pastors have stopped speaking the truth and started telling people what they want to hear. They are letting the fear of offending someone and losing their generous offering keep them from speaking the truth in love.

I often wonder how many of today's peace, love, and freewheeling grace preachers would quickly change their message if the money dried up. What if the donor base dwindled and went to someone else's more promising prophecy? I know what would happen. The change in cash flow would dictate: "If this potion of miracle medicine isn't selling anymore, then I'll find something that will." And of course, all said with a salesman's smile and guarantee of future success.

WE'RE PUTTING SKIERS AT RISK

So what should be happening when people come into the church? Let's go back to the analogy of the ski resort. Some are new at the sport of skiing and spend the majority of time in beginner's ski school just trying to keep their balance. New or novice skiers must begin on the bunny slope. They must learn how to stop. Often the most inviting method is snow plowing. Regardless, they *must* learn limitations. And of course, they must master the technique of turning. If not, they will be a threat to everyone on the slope.

It's the same in some churches. New Christians must first attend a beginner class so they can discover their position with Christ. The educational protocol is extremely important and often catches wolves before they embed themselves into the fold. Churches who do this have implemented wise spiritual steps. But it's grievous when these steps are bypassed.

Allow me to tell a little story to help illustrate my point.

My wife and I were launching out on our first day of skiing. We had rented all the gear and were ready to go. The ski instructor told us to rent shorter skis in order to turn easier. We refused because the longer ones looked cooler and matched our outfits. We were novices, the epitome of stupid.

Jeri had conquered stopping and knew how to turn and slow down. She was now ready to ride up the first lift and conquer the mini-mountain. We were in the Appalachians; it was sixty degrees. Thanks to an earlier storm there was still some snow and ice that we could ski on. Not good conditions for beginners. Most of the fresh stuff had melted into slush. The artificial snow-blowing machines were useless.

Only one portion of the mountain had enough icy snow that resembled a slope. Off to the left was grass and rock. We were there as youth pastors with one hundred young people. They had to ski, even if it was a potentially bad situation. We had traveled too far to turn back. Jeri made it off the lift, which is a triumphant feat for a beginner. She started sliding down the slope, but her skis quickly pointed in the wrong direction. Within a couple of minutes she flew off the thin slab of icy snow and hit grass, rock, and mud.

I was watching an experience unfold that we will never, ever forget. When her skis left the snow, they stopped—but she didn't. Her body kept flying, still bound to the skis. She completely flipped over, and her face slammed into the mud. The back of her skis flew up above and began banging her on the back of the head.

If you can't picture this, sorry. This was before the days of cell phones and tiny video cameras. There is no recording of this fabulous fiasco.

It was extremely funny and scary at the same time. She slid and slid through the mud while being battered on the back. Finally her body came to rest. Her face was completely covered in mud, her ski suit ruined from the fifty-foot slide down the slope. Man! Let's do that again.

Jeri recovered and eventually became a very good skier. Her memory of this event serves as a warning to all. Stay away from the mud.

You can take this tale and spiritualize it. Let's say that my wife is a new member of the church. She's just learning and willing to move forward. Like many new believers, she steps out in her new-found experience.

I say to all Christians. Stay on the slope. Stay away from muddy, murky teaching. Anything that doesn't appear to be pure, unadulterated spiritual snow... stay away. If you're not sure, then do some research. Don't just hang around "yes" people. Get around examiners who will test the waters. Heed what John said: "Beloved, do not believe every spirit, but test the spirits, whether they are of God; because many false prophets have gone out into the world" (1 John 4:1).

In many ski resorts novices are not allowed to advance until they've reached a level of competence. On the other hand, many churches often permit anyone to rise without questioning their spiritual capabilities, especially if they are high rollers. The perks are beyond anything God would permit. (Financial success will not be visited in this book due to the millions who suffer daily worldwide. I refuse to offend these brethren any more than they already are. We continue to minister in many of these countries and maintain good communication. Western success is measured by wealth, power, and people, while the majority of God's children measure His favor by their level of sacrifice and persecution. These men and women are recognized in this book's dedication.)

Satan is enticed by a novice with power. That is why so many churches produce reckless religious rioters. These people want their way or they'll split—or *cause* a split. Jezebels and Judases run rampant. Many unprepared skiers cause major harm to others just as many nondiscipled believers can wreak havoc in the body of Christ. We have made a mistake by not defining our welcome sign. Of course, come one, come all. But very shortly we must make it clear: *change* one, *change* all!

After you have finished reading this chapter, I trust that you now agree: we can no longer look the other way. We can no longer choose to do nothing. In the next chapter we'll discuss our obligation to respond to the call of this vision and save those in harm's way.

Chapter 4

NO GREATER OBLIGATION

THERE IS A GOOD POSSIBILITY THAT YOU AND I HAVE NEVER met. There is also a good possibility that you are not a novice. You have picked up this book because you want to know more about what to do to change the church and the society around us. •

We don't know each other, which raises the question, why should you trust me? Even though many respected leaders have provided endorsements for this book and I was mentored by some of the best, it still doesn't suffice. After all, there are countless books on the market endorsed by men and women who have backslidden, leaving a stain on the body of Christ. When you pick up a book and read a foreword from someone who has brought shame to Christ, His family, and their own family, it makes reading the book a bit difficult.

Perhaps I'm overreacting, perhaps not. Regardless, I want you to trust the words you've read and allow your spirit man to consume and digest the words to come. At times my expounding on the avalanche vision may seem judgmental. Please refrain from going there. It's not judgmental, and I'm not. I am writing as the Lord prompts.

I feel at times that I am actually taking dictation as God speaks. If you've ever written anything spiritual, a song, a sermon, or even a poem, you know exactly what I'm talking about. Sometimes you actually feel obligated to write, type, sing, or speak out the words God is giving. *Obligation* is a very serious word that means "to be bound legally or morally and to feel a strong commitment toward a certain act."

So I'm sending you via this book something that is obligatory. There is an inner, unwavering commitment to get the word out. And I hope you are sensing that you also have an obligation to hear what the Lord said and explore for yourself what you should be doing.

When you find a certain subject being repeated several times in various ways, it is not an editorial error. By discussing heresies over and over, the truth begins to sink in. The good seed begins to take root. In time this tree will bear faith-filled fruit. You'll be so glad that time was taken to uproot the weeds and plant His words.

I only have a few hours, or perhaps a few days, with you before this book will be read, shelved, and you move on. My goal is that, though it may find its way onto the bookshelf, the words will have found their way into your heart. And of course, it's best for it not to collect dust. Pass it on. You'll find the writing is perpetual, not dated. The subject matter of the vision will be relevant for years to come.

Before I move on, I am compelled to add the following scripture to edify and encourage you for two reasons. The first is that the devil lost, we won! The second is that you will overcome!

> Then I heard a loud voice saying in heaven, "Now salvation, and strength, and the kingdom of our God, and the power of His Christ have come, for the accuser of our brethren, who

accused them before our God day and night, has been cast down. And they overcame him by the blood of the Lamb and by the word of their testimony, and they did not love their lives to the death."

—REVELATION 12:10–11

Throughout this book you will read of the urgency of the hour. Thank God, we still have some light to do the work. "I must work the works of him that sent me, while it is day: the night cometh, when no man can work" (John 9:4, KJV).

From the moment I first shared this vision, leaders worldwide have been calling and writing, wanting to know what their part should be in this impending disaster. The answer, for everyone, can be found in these pages. I have certainly been put in *my* place by this revelation and trust you will be too.

LET'S CLARIFY A FEW THINGS

When someone meets the qualifications of the title "ski patrol," there are certain obligations that are in concrete. Immovable. Beyond discussion. This is where I live as a revivalist, where you should live regardless of your earthly title, and where these men and women live who patrol the mountains.

The members of the ski patrol are obligated to:

- Care for skiers

- Be responsible in every area of their lives

- Be dependable

- Ski all the dangerous terrain

- Stay with a wounded skier

- Keep their family strong

- Administer first aid

- Stay trained in their profession

- Stay up-to-date in technology

- Fulfill their assignments

- Maintain their skills

- Keep skiers safe

- Risk their lives to save others

- And much, much more!

Do you see the incredible similarity between these rangers and God's soldiers?

We are obligated to use the one tool that will rescue lost souls: the blessed good news. Christ crucified. The hard-hitting facts of the basic gospel will produce bountiful fruit. "For if I preach the gospel, I have nothing to boast of, for necessity is laid upon me; yes, woe is me if I do not preach the gospel!" (1 Cor. 9:16).

Let's consider a few obligations we're familiar with:

- A good father is obligated to take care of and provide for his family.

- A good mother feels an obligation to care for and nurture her children.

- A pilot is obligated to the passengers on his aircraft and is committed to making sure they arrive safely at their destination.

- A committed schoolteacher is obligated to impart knowledge to the students.

- A trustworthy politician is obligated to the voters and committed to fulfilling all campaign promises.

- A doctor is obligated to the health and well-being of his or her patients.

- A fireman is obligated to not only putting out fires but also rescuing those who may perish in the flames.

Whom are you obligated to? The answer is your Savior, the One who saved you. You were perishing and He reached out and rescued you. He saved you. He saved me. That's why we call Him Savior.

IT'S A MATTER OF LIFE AND DEATH

Could you imagine being covered in ten feet of snow on the backside of a mountain with only minutes to live? Most of us can't fathom that kind of certain death. You might somehow carve a small oxygen pocket around your mouth, but that only buys a few more moments of life.

Then the unthinkable happens. You feel a jab in your back. It's the pointed, steel tip of an avalanche probe. At the other end is a ranger obligated to save your life. Once he hits your body, the shovel is pulled out and the frantic digging begins. You are trying to compose your elation to conserve every molecule of lifesaving air. Then, a few minutes later, you see light. The drama is over. You've survived the most treacherous event of your life.

The ranger, in the secular sense of the word, is a savior. He saved you from certain death. From that moment on, and for the rest of your life, you will no doubt feel an obligation to that man. He may refuse your attention, but you will never stop thanking him.

Now you are so affected by his commitment to save others that you decide to become a member of the ski patrol yourself. You know it takes a lot to qualify.

Are you seeing the parallel in the spiritual world? The demands on true Christians will never be more than we can handle, but it will take a commitment that is hard to find in today's church world.

Those who are going to help destroy these potential avalanches must be willing to take swift and accurate action. We must be spiritually fit and willing to penetrate the danger zones. Armed with our weapons of warfare and obligated to carry out the mission, we advance.

> **The demands on true Christians will never be more than we can handle, but it will take a commitment that is hard to find in today's church world.**

TEST YOUR QUALIFICATIONS

Now, take a test. Below I've shown the parallel between the qualifications of the ski patrol and our spiritual qualifications. Are you ready? (Of course, those of you reading this book who are not fully committed to Jesus, just relax. Read every page. There's good news for you coming soon.)

A ski patrolman or ranger has a physically demanding job; ours is a spiritually demanding job. I've already shared the obligations, but now here are the qualifications questionnaires.

Ranger

- Can you ski the toughest, most extreme terrain?

- Are you able to administer first aid?

- Can you maneuver a sled to carry the wounded to safety?

- Are you physically fit?

- Do you have a basic understanding of the types of snow?

- Are you up-to-date on avalanche science?

Christian

- Can you face the toughest spiritual heresies?

- Are you able to help those who have fallen prey?

- Can you take the critical spiritually wounded to a more qualified, equipped group of deliverance intercessors?

- Are you spiritually fit today?

- Do you understand the types of false teaching and how they deceive the flock?

- Are you up-to-date on what is coming in the end times?

Jesus is the One who delivered you from darkness and allows you to live in His marvelous light. If this has truly happened to you, if Christ is truly your Savior, then once again there is a certain obligation that befalls you.

If you say you love Jesus, then you will do the things He asks of you. That's why I received this vision and I'm willing to share it worldwide. It doesn't matter if people hate me or love me. I am obligated to Him and Him alone. My commitment is to Jesus.

I can feel the Spirit of the Lord as I write. There are some who are reading right now with tears dripping on the pages. You have wavered in your commitment, but that's over. Right now you're back! You're back with an unquenchable zeal. Nothing will keep you from moving forward! You will no longer be afraid of man; you will fear only God. The fear of God is an all-consuming reverence of Him. It is the foundation of everything. When you fear Him, you begin to understand His plans. When you fear Him, you obey Him.

It is the fundamental fear of God that causes me to push forward, regardless of what people think. When the battle is over, you will stand before Him, alone. I will stand before Him, alone. It's not a buddy system. Your critics won't be there. They will stand face-to-face before Jesus, alone.

THE MANDATES OF THE WORD

To carry out the mandate in the vision, we must carry out the mandates of the Word. While reading the following, please don't skip over the scriptures. When you jump over the Word, you are bypassing God. He always gets the first and final say.

> The fear of the LORD is the beginning of knowledge,
> But fools despise wisdom and instruction.
> —PROVERBS 1:7

> The fear of man brings a snare,
> But whoever trusts in the LORD shall be safe.
> —PROVERBS 29:25

You've broken out of the trap, the fear of man is gone, and the fear of God has consumed you with a vengeance.

> For God has not given us a spirit of fear, but of power and of love and of a sound mind. Therefore do not be ashamed of the

testimony of our Lord, nor of me His prisoner, but share with me in the sufferings for the gospel according to the power of God, who has saved us and called us with a holy calling, not according to our works, but according to His own purpose and grace which was given to us in Christ Jesus before time began, but has now been revealed by the appearing of our Savior Jesus Christ, who has abolished death and brought life and immortality to light through the gospel.

—2 Timothy 1:7–10

I'm overjoyed that you have abolished the fear of man and have acknowledged the fear of God. This is fundamental equipment for the work ahead.

Praise the Lord!
Blessed is the man who fears the Lord,
Who delights greatly in His commandments.

—Psalm 112:1

Now, love Him!

If you love Me, keep My commandments.

—John 14:15

You are now obligated to take care of His business. If I were the head of the ski patrol, my orders would be "Hit the slopes!"
Jesus said:

Go ye into all the world, and preach the gospel to every creature.

—Mark 16:15, kjv

I'm sure people would love for Jesus to have covered other topics, such as "a free ride to heaven," or "now that you're saved, you don't

49

have to behave," or "the judgments are through, they're not for you," or "it's a holiday; take My Word and throw it away," or "don't look to Me for the end-time plan; the Antichrist is coming, he's your man," or "you don't have to share with humanity lost; they're all saved without a cost."

I could go on and on, but the fact is, without a doubt, these were the furthest from His mind. He was committed to burning His passion for souls into the hearts of the disciples. And that's why He said, "Go." My friend, does that two-letter word impact you?

That's right, we need to have a burning, passionate obligation to our neighbor.

I thank God that Jesus Christ felt obligated to His neighbor. Why? Because I am the neighbor! You are the neighbor. Everyone caught up in the spiritual fallacies of today are our neighbors.

Where's our obligation?

When ski patrols go out in the dead of night to hunt down danger, no one knows who they are. The skiers are safe in the lodge, log cabins, and condos. They're sipping hot coffee around a roaring fire. They glance out the window and are oblivious to those dark figures with lights scurrying up the mountain. I know what I'm talking about because I've been by the fireside, safe and secure, while they are laying everything down, obligated to my safety.

Members of the ski patrol are often nameless, faceless figures fighting for those who often have no appreciation for their job. Welcome to the ministry. Welcome to this vision.

Are you willing to act like these ski patrol? See what the apostle Paul said:

> Let this mind be in you which was also in Christ Jesus, who, being in the form of God, did not consider it robbery to be equal with God, but made Himself of no reputation, taking

the form of a bondservant, and coming in the likeness of men. And being found in appearance as a man, He humbled Himself and became obedient to the point of death, even the death of the cross.

—PHILIPPIANS 2:5–8

Are you willing to live a life of "no reputation" like Christ? Are you committed to reaching out to those who can't give anything in return?

Determine to be a nameless, faceless figure, a follower of no reputation, willing to fight for the millions who so desperately need you. Read on, and I will teach you how if you will make that vow.

Chapter 5

A GOOD NIGHT'S SLEEP

A GOOD NIGHT'S SLEEP IS MANDATORY FOR A GOOD DAY OF skiing. This Alpine sport is not only demanding on the body but also equally on the mind. To be mentally alert while flying down the slopes at twenty to fifty miles per hour is crucial to a skier's safety and that of others. That is the reason why many die in accidents, slamming into trees or other obstacles.

A skier must be healthy in every sense of the word. The same with a God-fearing Christian. Paul said, "Remind them of these things, charging them before the Lord not to strive about words to no profit, to the ruin of the hearers. Be diligent to present yourself approved to God, a worker who does not need to be ashamed, rightly dividing the word of truth. But shun profane and idle babblings, for they will increase to more ungodliness" (2 Tim. 2:14–16).

We must be knowledgeable in the Word, able to wield our weapons, and have a fresh relationship with Jesus. We are commanded to be sober and alert, or we could slam into obstacles that destroy us spiritually: "Therefore let us not sleep, as others do, but let us watch and be sober. For those who sleep, sleep at night, and those who get drunk are drunk at night. But let us who are of the day be sober, putting on the breastplate of faith and love, and as a helmet the hope of salvation" (1 Thess. 5:6–8). Of course in this letter the apostle Paul was not speaking of physical sleep but was referring to being awake spiritually. Sadly, as in the vision, the present, awe-inspiring teachings have lulled many into a deep spiritual sleep.

In the vision, while the skiers slept, the snow began to fall. The amount of snow that fell during the storm was alarming to the ski patrol. That is why they were put on full alert and geared up. Their heavy weaponry in the vision dictated the intensity of the war ahead. They were preparing for the worst.

All it takes for an avalanche is a layer of snow and a slope for it to slide down. Sounds so simple. How could something so fluffy, so powdery, so clean and white be so deadly? It's time to stop *questioning* the facts and start *following* the facts. How can a teaching so soft and so gentle have in its future the spiritual suffocation of so many saints?

Snowfall is so different from rain or hail. A torrential rainstorm or a violent hail downpour can cause sleepers to run for safety. The sound of hail pelting the roof and destroying the car will awaken the deepest sleeper. Hearing chunks of ice the size of golf balls pelt the ground can keep you up all night.

On the other hand snow is almost silent and allows a skier to sleep soundly, undisturbed. I am again weeping over how long this sickness has kept me in a state of slumber. I was a soldier, sleeping through the snowstorm, unable to fight.

MY RECENT BRUSH WITH DEATH

I mentioned earlier in this book my deliverance from the valley of the shadow of death. I had been battling melanoma cancer for many years. There was no medical cure for advanced stages of this disease. They call it "the killer," and rightfully so. If it weren't for Jesus, my loving wife, and the prayers of the saints, I would not be writing today.

After several chemo treatments that took years off my life, my body totally gave up. My vital organs shut down, and I was given a few days to live. Jeri bought two burial plots and planned my funeral. The rest is an incredible story.

During the darkest nights of this physical trial I was completely disoriented. I didn't know my wife's name, the year, where I lived, my age, birth date—everything was gone. One psychiatrist said that I had lost over 80 percent of my memory. I believed him. It was so hard and so sad. Here I was, a man who had prayed for hundreds of thousands. I'd seen miracles worldwide. Now, it was my turn.

No one knows how many days they will live. Moses asked the Lord to help him number his days. "The days of our lives are seventy years; and if by reason of strength they are eighty years, yet their boast is only labor and sorrow; for it is soon cut off, and we fly away. Who knows the power of Your anger? For as the fear of You, so is Your wrath. So teach us to number our days, that we may gain a heart of wisdom" (Ps. 90:10–12).

We will all go sometime and somehow. I believe in total healing through the work of Jesus on Calvary and claim my right to that suffering every day. You should too! Be healed, in Jesus' name!

I'm sharing this for a purpose. During an extended period of time it was like I was in a deep, dark sleep. I can remember a lot of details, such as midnight ambulance trips to the emergency room, late-night visits from nurses trying to save my life, and other events that somehow have been retained. But the rest of the years are as if I had been detached from reality.

The return to life was slow, the details too numerous to record in this book. But one incredible detail must be shared in this chapter. You see, for many years I was out of touch with Christendom. It was as if I was in a comatose state and everything was passing me by. Taking care of the killer disease was priority. It consumed all our time and a lot of money. Without our friends we would not have made it.

It was as if I was asleep and years later woke up. Upon waking, I discovered that the church, in just a few short years, had fallen into a state that seemed irreparable. So much hype, so little hope. So much laughter, so little weeping. So much freedom, so little sacrifice. So much teaching, so little transformation. So much preaching, so little passion.

When I woke, it was shocking to see how far the church had fallen. Please don't grow angry with me. There's no purpose in that. I'm not angry with anyone. I am seeing clearly the state of affairs, and we need repairs. Of course there are on-fire Jesus-filled churches. There are millions who are serving the Lord. There are some incredible humble, sacrificial pastors and lay leaders. But don't ever stop there. The world is desperately seeking a Savior. Why can't we get Him to them? What on earth is holding us back?

It was like being away from family for years then coming back to see how much they'd grown and changed. Sometimes we reunite with family and everything is great. Other times their new ungodly friends and hurtful, hellish habits sadden us.

Well, I am awake! This spiritual skier has had a good night's sleep.

Now I look out the window and see what's been happening during the night hours. It all relates so strongly to this chapter.

Once the skiers have had a peaceful night's rest, then it's time to energize the body with a good breakfast, layer up, buckle up the boots, strap on the skis, grab the goggles, head out the door, and hit the slopes. On any given day you may choose smooth, graceful powder (some call it the "milk run"), a demanding battle with the moguls, or a more daring flight down the best of the black diamonds. Maybe dodging the evergreens through the woods is your idea of a great run. It's up to the skier, and all makes for an incredible day. To an avid skier every dollar is well spent.

IT'S TIME TO GET DRESSED!

The skier knows that he cannot attack the slopes until he is properly outfitted for the challenges ahead. The clothes one would wear on the street are of no use on the mountain. The winter warrior must put on the right "armor" if they are to stay warm and safe for the day ahead.

A good ski shop will help a new skier acquire the proper attire. Paul gives us our "equipment checklist" in Ephesians 6.

> Put on the whole armor of God, that you may be able to stand against the wiles of the devil. For we do not wrestle against flesh and blood, but against principalities, against powers, against the rulers of the darkness of this age, against spiritual hosts of wickedness in the heavenly places. Therefore take up the whole armor of God, that you may be able to withstand in the evil day, and having done all, to stand.
>
> —EPHESIANS 6:11–13

The body was not made to survive in the bitter cold that accompanies the mountain. Likewise, you and I cannot survive in this fallen world unprotected from the devices and schemes of a very real enemy who wants to see you overtaken!

The skier begins with a proper base layer of clothing sufficient to meet the forecast temperatures of the day. A pair of ski pants, a jacket, and pair of gloves ensure the cold wet snow stays on the outside. Likewise, Christ's righteousness and His truth become our insulator from the world. Paul tells us to "stand therefore, having girded your waist with truth, having put on the breastplate of righteousness" (v. 14). We are robed in His righteousness and are protected by His truth. In Him is the only safe place to be!

Once skiers are properly dressed, they strap themselves into their boots. Walking in a pair of ski boots is very awkward, but that's because walking is not their purpose. They are designed to make the skier one with the skis and secure the ankles from twisting during a demanding descent. Our spiritual feet must be secure as well. We are instructed, "Shod your feet with the preparation of the gospel of peace" (v. 15). We go where He wants us to go. We stay where He wants us to stay. We become one with Him, always ready to take the good news of the gospel where He leads.

An item that seems burdensome to novice skiers is their poles. They don't understand their purpose—that is, until they've lost them. I've watched quite a few skiers struggle to get down the mountain without them. The poles help the skier keep his balance while standing and skiing. Jesus has given us all the equipment we need to stand firm. I love that Paul encourages us, saying, "Above all, taking the shield of faith with which you will be able to quench all the fiery darts of the wicked one" (v. 16). Faith is our defense. It enables us to stand in the midst of any trial or test life will throw our way.

The skier protects his head with a warm hat and a pair of goggles. This is vital to keep the head warm and his vision clear. Keeping your head protected is vital! We need to "take the helmet of salvation" (v. 17). The enemy is going to play every possible mind game with you that he can. He will throw every possible thought and image your way to cloud your judgment and cause you to stumble. That's why we must let our mind be renewed by washing it thoroughly with God's Word.

The skier's weapon of choice for attacking the snow is either a pair of snow skis or a snowboard. With them the skier is able to slice through the snow just like a razor through a sheet. It is important for us as believers to take "the sword of the Spirit, which is the word of God; praying always with all prayer and supplication in the Spirit, being watchful to this end with all perseverance and supplication for all the saints" (vv. 17–18).

Believers must be able to swing the sword of God's Word with great skill and accuracy as they face the challenges that await them each day. Know the Word! Speak the Word! Pray the Word! We do not fight as the world fights. Our weapon is God's Word, and what a powerful weapon it is! As you can see, there is an insightful comparison of our spiritual armor with the skier's gear.

REMEMBER THE CODES

If a skier is planning on hitting the slopes (or *pistes*), he must be cognizant of the simple mandatory rules of skiing. These rules are amazingly applicable to Christian living. Once you've put on the necessary ski gear or spent time putting on the whole armor of God, look at some well-orchestrated instructions that will help you enjoy your run and, of course, assure you of a successful Christian life.

Here are some of the codes of skiing (with their spiritual parallels in italics):

1. Ski safely, not only for yourself but for others as well. *Live your Christian life not only for yourself but for others as well.*
2. Always stay in control and be able to stop or avoid objects. *As a Christian, always stay alert and be ready to stop and evaluate what may lie ahead.*
3. People ahead of you have the right of way. It is your responsibility to avoid them. *Don't spend your Christian life running over others. Humble yourself, and He will move you forward in due time.*
4. Whenever starting downhill or merging onto a trail, yield to others. *As a Christian, look at others as more important than yourself.*
5. Observe all posted signs and warnings. *Observe all the rules and regulations in the Word.*
6. Keep off closed trails and out of closed areas. *Believers should stay away from any areas that may detour them into potential traps set up by the enemy.*

Christians should make sure their foundation is laid strong and their spiritual house can withstand the storm that *will* come. Don't allow yourself to be blown around by any new wind of doctrine. Maintain control of your Christian life.

Control is an important slope-safety issue. To stay in control, you must ski in terrain areas within your ability range. Just as the driver must know how to step on the brakes if someone crosses in front of the car, a skier needs to know how to stop if a person is crossing the path.

Christians must learn how to stop. *Selah!* That word means to stop and think about it. We are to be awake, with full armor, ready for the battle ahead, just as the skier is to be alert, fully equipped for the slopes, ready to face any unexpected event.

DON'T SLEEP THROUGH THE ALARM

The sounds of alarm that originate in heaven come to Christendom demanding our immediate attention. These warnings and signs of dangerous times can appear at a moment's notice. Likewise it is critical that sleepy skiers hear the alarms of imminent danger because those alarms may determine whether they will live or die.

While we sleep, the blizzard of deception is falling. The devil isn't sleeping; he's working overtime, dumbing down the skiers. They are so inebriated that by morning their hangover fogs the ski patrol's instructions.

The devil further amplifies these conditions by adding the physical state of too little sleep. A tired body and a sluggish brain are a sure formula for disaster on the slopes. Add in the impending avalanche, and the devil is going to win, despite all warnings and teachings.

> **While we sleep, the blizzard of deception is falling.**

Spiritually speaking, many people die from the lack of common sense. Their judgment is impaired to the point that it may cost them their lives when the avalanche cascades down the mountain. Every Sunday morning they dreamily head off to the house of God after a peaceful night's rest. Depending on the church, they either put on their best for some full-blown, robed choir and grab a hymnal for high church or they slip on their favorite tie-dyed tee, shorts, and sandals for the church where "you can come as you are."

I'm not here to bash one church's style of worship over another's. What I am here to do is wake up Christians from their sleepy haze so that when they sit in the next service, they will have sharp minds, fully awake, ready to discern the message that's being served to them. Like a fresh blanket of new snow, it might look and sound beautiful, but don't be deceived. In the next chapter we'll take a look at how the snow can cover dangerous terrain and trick the untrained eye.

Chapter 6

EVERYTHING LOOKS SO BEAUTIFUL

I
T'S A BRAND-NEW DAY! LOOKING OUT THE WINDOW, WE SEE
nothing but white. While we were sleeping in the night, a storm
front blew in, dumping a foot of fresh snow on the mountain. What
a dream come true! Excitement is in the air. It's why we came to the
resort. The skiers understand the joy of the sport. Their minds are
not concerned over what's beneath the blanket. Powder snow is the
ideal base for most snowboarders and skiers. Although this pillowy
surface makes for a perfect run, it can also cover rocks, ice, tree
stumps, and other dangerous obstacles. That's why you have to stay
alert and keep your eyes wide open.

My most memorable wipeouts have come when I was just
enthralled with the ride without being alert to what might lie
beneath. In the same way, Christians rarely concern themselves
over the depth of any teaching. Why waste time examining the
prophet and his prophecy? That's already been done. Just enjoy the
benefits. Enjoy the view. Love the music. Look at what's falling. It's
new. It's fresh! It's now! The old is gone.

We can't wait to worship atop the spiritual mountain. The

tantalizing teachers have tickled us beyond belief. The new wave of worship has us penetrating the heavens with praise. What we fail to understand is that what appears to be spiritual food could actually be starving the spirit man. Satan was completely caught up in this heavenly realm, yet his experiences led him to deception and the damning dominance of his converts. Their destiny is a smoldering death.

In this book we'll take an educational journey through some of the world's most destructive avalanches, and I think you'll see something fascinating. The most horrific heresies blowing through the landscape of today's church are not unlike the incredible snowstorms that have destroyed lives and properties over the centuries.

> **Joining a church doesn't make you a Christian any more than going to the Olympics makes you a star athlete.**

Yes, everything looks so beautiful. But what lies beneath? Where are the deadly danger zones that cause catastrophic casualties and create the conditions for that killer avalanche?

First, let's start with the basics. The whole foundation of Christianity is built on Christ and Him crucified. According to the apostle Paul, "No other foundation can anyone lay than that which is laid, which is Jesus Christ" (1 Cor. 3:11). Sadly, multitudes believe only that Jesus is the Son of God and that He died on the cross for our sins. But that's it. They don't understand what it means to be saved, that we must be born again. My friend, joining a church doesn't make you a Christian any more than going to the Olympics makes you a star athlete.

So here's one of the dangers permeating many evangelical and full gospel churches today. In an effort to make Christianity appealing and comfortable, in a desire to be inclusive and ecumenical, scores of pastors are not proclaiming from the pulpit that we must be born again. So many sitting in the pews don't realize that they need to be saved, that they need to have their sins forgiven.

This resembles the skiing experience of a friend of mine. She recounts:

As I was growing up in a northern region of the United States, winter sports were a way of life for us. It wasn't until my sophomore year in high school, however, that I had my first experience snow skiing. My cousins traveled to Michigan for a ski trip and invited me to come along. Experienced skiers would consider the slopes in Southern Michigan to be bunny hills at best. But for a beginner like me, it was a perfect introduction to this exhilarating sport. After a few minutes of instruction from my "expert" cousins, I was sailing down the slopes having the time of my life. I was hooked!

The following year I convinced my parents to buy me a set of skis for Christmas. I was now "officially" a skier. No, I never joined the ski club, never took lessons, and over the course of the next few years I skied just a handful of times. But I proudly wore the badge of skier, enjoying the persona and the novelty of the idea, because few, if any, of my friends could say that they were skiers.

A few years later when I moved away for college, my skis wound up in my parents' attic and were eventually sold in a garage sale. So what happened to my passion for my favorite winter sport? Quite simply this: When I was in high school, my parents bought my skis, my gear, my lift tickets, my transportation to the ski resorts, and even my meals. It didn't cost me a thing. All I had to do was put on my skis and have fun. But now that I was on my own, I had to put forth time, effort, and pay—even save—my own money to go skiing. So I quickly lost interest and hung up my skis to pursue other interests.

Skiing became a thing of the past until a decade later when my husband and I ventured to the spectacular slopes of Squaw Valley, California, where the 1960 Winter Olympics were held. Riding that scenic aerial tram to the 8,200-foot High Camp, I quickly realized that skiing on mountains was a totally different experience than skiing on bunny hills. On the hills I traveled down the well-worn paths of other skiers, making everything easy. On the mountain I had to navigate deep powder snow, blazing my own trail. I repeatedly toppled over my own skis that were buried under several feet of fresh-fallen snow. And I can't tell you how many times my husband and I collided because he couldn't figure out how to turn, let alone stop.

Yet what an experience! Exhilarating? Yes! But it was also frustrating and exhausting, not to mention that we suffered a few bumps and bruises from our many tumbles. Thankfully we had no broken bones! Clearly, to be safe and to experience skiing the way it was meant to be, we needed more than the quick one-hour lesson we took at the beginning of our day. Had we stuck with it and applied ourselves, our whole experience and outlook would have been different. But as it was, our schedule only permitted one day on the slopes, so once again I hung up my passion for skiing, uncertain if I would ever pursue it again.

My friend's experience with skiing resembles the experience many have with Christianity. Someone invites them to church. Wow! They've never encountered anything like that before. So they buy a Bible, start visiting the church, and maybe, just maybe, respond to an altar call. Then they start making some friends and perhaps go to a class or two.

Everything is great for a while. Going to church makes them feel good. From the awesome music, the speaker, the friendliness of the people…everything is beautiful. All is going well until this new Christian encounters a test or trial in life.

They hit some rocky terrain on the ski slopes of life. Unprepared, they take some tumbles, acquire some bruises, and then begin to question this whole thing called "Christianity." Next thing you know, they throw in the towel, saying that this Christian stuff is too tough. It costs too much. It requires too much effort. They just can't live the life. Nobody told them they had to change, to repent of sin, or that it would require effort on their part to grow in the things of God. So they disappear. Sadly their Bible ends up on the shelf, collecting dust.

Let me remind you of something I talked about in chapter 3: although some churches are prepared to take care of new converts, the danger comes when these new believers are not given the whole story. The crucified life is a challenging life. Contrary to much of the snowy teaching, major trials confront these new Christians, catching them totally off guard.

I spend much of my life teaching Western Christians to put their beliefs in a global context. While we may see everything as beautiful, there are billions around the world who see it in a completely different way. They know that serving Christ could mean not only excommunication from family and friends but also often physical death. For this reason this avalanche vision has taken on international appeal. It makes sense to those who are living the sacrificial life.

Jesus spoke of this very thing when He told the parable of the sower. The sower went out to sow seed. Some seed fell by the way-side, some on the stony places, some among thorns, and some on good ground. He explained the parable by saying:

> When anyone hears the word of the kingdom, and does not understand it, then the wicked one comes and snatches away what was sown in his heart. This is he who received seed by the wayside. But he who received the seed on stony places, this is he who hears the word and immediately receives it with joy; yet he has no root in himself, but endures only for a while. For when tribulation or persecution arises because of the word, immediately he stumbles. Now he who received seed among the thorns is he who hears the word, and the cares of this world and the deceitfulness of riches choke the word, and he becomes unfruitful. But he who received seed on the good ground is he who hears the word and understands it, who indeed bears fruit and produces: some a hundredfold, some sixty, some thirty.
>
> —Matthew 13:19–23

Our responsibility as ministers of the gospel is to preach and teach the truth so the hearers become rooted and grounded in the faith. We must equip them to handle treacherous terrain that they will encounter on the challenging slopes of life.

We start by uncovering layers of snow that are piled on this mountain called Christianity. Let's explore some more snow-covered slopes.

EXPLORING THE LAYERS

I'll never forget the time I went to a Christmas production at a large church. I was invited by a friend, and he told me excitedly about all the makings of the production—the hard work that went into it, the money spent, the time involved. The place was packed to capacity. It was obvious that many people had come who were away from God. The performance was spectacular, and the gospel message was clearly portrayed through the Christmas story. By the end of the drama hearts were open and tender. You felt it. So you can imagine my shock when the pastor got up and said to the crowd, "Wasn't that a great production? Give everybody a hand." He then wished the people a merry Christmas and dismissed the service. I was in shock. It was obvious that many at the musical were not right with God. People around me were actually weeping. I expected an altar call where these people would have the opportunity to soak the carpet with their tears and get right with God on this blessed night.

As an evangelist I always think to myself, "What if a sinner attending this service has a car accident and dies on his way home tonight?" I received a letter from a precious godly mother who thanked me for my direct appeal for lost souls. Her son was dramatically saved in one of our meetings. He called her from the church to let her know of his radical transformation. He headed home, and I would imagine he couldn't wait to tell all his friends and family. That never happened. In her grieving letter she thanked me for being bold. It was just what her son needed. He got saved, and a few hours later he was in heaven.

I deeply grieve over the countless souls who are lost for eternity because "we're too busy with our programs," or "it doesn't fit in with our message," or "we don't want to embarrass anybody."

So, just like today's ski resorts that create bunny-slope environments to make everyone feel like a skier, in the spiritual we make everyone feel as if they are saved. This is a layer of what theologians call "universal reconciliation." It's a dream come true for everyone, but in actuality it's a nightmare in the making.

Throughout these pages we'll uncover more tantalizing teachings of dangerous snow.

"There is a way that seems right to a man, but its end is the way of death" (Prov. 14:12). This passage gives us the warning to check out "the way" and see if it conforms to the Word. We could compare this to the skier who hears his buddies telling him to go down a certain slope. The rumor at the resort is that it's great. Upon consulting a map, though, he discovers that the slope is listed as black, meaning it's dangerous and only for advanced skiers, or that a particular slope is considered impassable. Woe to the snow bunny who listens to the other skiers and pays no heed to the warning on the map. What seems like a thrilling ride could lead to an accident or even death.

The novice skier seems to be the one at fault for taking a slope that's wrong for him. If he's been properly taught, then certainly he's responsible if he chooses not to heed the instructions and warnings. But what about the ski master, the teacher, who failed to drill into the student the dos and don'ts of safe skiing? Check the maps; ask the experts; when in doubt, wait. These are the golden rules of safety, and no novice should hit the slopes without learning them. Certainly the instructor who fails to properly prepare his pupils for the slopes bears culpability.

The avalanche vision lays the blame on these instructors. This is a direct word from the Lord with no compromise. Faithful leaders around the country and the world are calling in with thanksgiving for the clarity of these words. One pastor took total responsibility for leading his church astray, and I trust thousands will follow.

The Word tells us that teachers will be judged by a higher standard and with greater severity than others: "My brethren, let not many of you become teachers, knowing that we shall receive a stricter judgment" (James 3:1). This warning should cause every leader to carefully consider how they instruct others and how they live their lives.

Countless people are falling into the worldly abyss as they leave church services and walk back into the real world of pitfalls, obstacles, and enticements. They have no firm foundation to combat the wiles of Satan and overcome the world. Just as we must have a firmly packed snow base to make a successful ski run, so we must have a solid spiritual base to enable us to swoop down the slopes of life and stay clear of the enemy and his diabolical plans.

> **Many leave a church service feeling good about themselves instead of feeling fantastic about God.**

"But it's so beautiful," the skier sighs. "It looks like so much fun." Yes, it would be fun until the skier crashes into a hidden tree stump or falls into a crevasse. The Bible doesn't say we should live by feelings but "by every word of God" (Luke 4:4). Feelings are deceptive because they are of the soul, not the spirit.

The "I'm okay" teachings of today generate feelings of self-worth, which are like mistaken feelings of "I'm a good skier." Could it be true that many leave a church service feeling good about themselves instead of feeling fantastic about God?

The Bible warns us that Satan appears as an angel of light: "Satan himself transforms himself into an angel of light. Therefore it is no great thing if his ministers also transform themselves into ministers of righteousness, whose end will be according to their works" (2 Cor. 11:14–15).

We've all heard the heart-rending stories of the girl who married the man of her dreams, only to discover he's a violent spouse abuser; the man who takes on a business partner, only to find out that the partner steals him blind; the elected officials who break all their campaign promises; the children lured away by a sex offender; the people in authority—perhaps a counselor, an educator, a coach, or a church leader—who sexually violate the very ones they pledge to protect and help. These are all examples of Satan disguising himself as an angel of light.

Meet Theresa. She was one of the most intelligent girls in our youth group. She was a few years older, in her late twenties, but we all enjoyed listening to her wisdom. She knew the Bible better than all of us. We had regular fellowship meetings in which she always had something to say. She was a spiritual dynamo.

But then she disappeared. A few weeks went by, no Theresa. Then a couple months, still a no-show. Several of us who were leading the Bible study became increasingly concerned. We hunted her down and found that she had joined another Bible study. Everything she shared was not only biblical but also exciting. Her face radiated with Jesus. We were saddened that she was gone but happy that she was with another good, strong group of believers.

Two years went by. On a Sunday morning she came walking in the back door. Several of us greeted her, but something was different. Her joy was gone. Her smile was fabricated. It didn't take long before we realized that Theresa had joined a cult. She had lost everything—her savings account, her car, many of her possessions, all gone.

She began to pour out one of the most heart-wrenching stories that I had ever heard. I was a young Christian, growing in God and also learning the deceptive ways of Satan. For Theresa, everything at the beginning was so beautiful. There was enough truth, like snow, to cover the ground. What was underneath were demonic ideas that would destroy that young life. She had almost sold out completely when deep in her spirit she felt that the end would be devastating. Jesus was speaking to her. She wept and wept years of tears. She came home that day and was a warning to all of us that just because something looks right doesn't mean it is right. Oh, did I tell you that Theresa was a graduate of a major Bible school and had a degree in theology? Even the most spiritual, intelligent Christians can be led astray.

Perhaps you've been deceived by someone who said all the right things but who was all the wrong things. You're not alone! No matter how young or how old we are, no matter how spiritually mature, no matter how many years we've been in the ministry, none of us is immune to deception.

Those who are trained to spot counterfeit money say that the best way to recognize the fake is by handling the real. The more they handle real money, paying close attention to how it feels in their hands, studying the details of each bill, the more often they can spot the fake just by touching it. Likewise our place of safety is to be solidly grounded in the Word, to obey His Word, to listen to the Holy Spirit (who will never lead you apart from the Word), and to heed wise counsel.

The devil has nothing new. He packages his lies with just enough truth, just enough Jesus to lure people away, just enough snow to cover the dangers beneath. Many think they are the exception to the rule. That they can play with fire and not get burned. That they can ignore the danger signs on the slippery slopes and not end up in peril. That they can skate on thin ice and not fall through. That they can play with sin and not be destroyed. "It will never happen to me," they think. My friend, "Let him who thinks he stands take heed lest he fall" (1 Cor. 10:12).

Like the enthusiastic skiers caught up in the beauty of the winter wonderland resort, so many believers are being swept away by trappings of the tinsel teachings of today, not realizing they're being drawn away from that straight and narrow path.

In the next chapter I'll expose several false teachings that are prevalent in the church today so that you can begin to discern the messages you are listening to. Don't be fooled by fresh snow that is covering up the dangerous lies of teachings that do not line up with God's Word. Read on and ask for the Holy Spirit's help as you seek the truth.

Chapter 7

WHITEOUT

Jeri and I were traveling through the southern state of Georgia on the interstate, going over seventy miles per hour, when we were overcome by a white cloud of windblown snow. Jeri shouted out, "Steve, it's snowing!" This was very unusual for that part of the country. Georgia isn't known for extreme winter weather, so when Old Man Winter rears his ugly head, most are unprepared.

I shouted out, "I can't see! I can't see a thing." We were experiencing a complete whiteout. I don't remember ever being so afraid. I lost all sense of direction. Though my speedometer said how fast I was going, I felt I was standing still. I couldn't see the road. I couldn't see other cars. Everything had vanished, replaced by this strange, mystical white. The only thing I knew to do was to slow down and pray that I was still on the road.

When I finally came to a stop, I was off the road on the median. All we could do was wait out the storm. Time seemed to stand still. What felt like hours really only took ten minutes. When the storm lifted, I finally saw what we had gone through. Miles in front of me and miles behind me were wrecks—too many to number. Massive trucks had slid off the road and turned over. Cars were everywhere. How we survived I will never know, outside of the hand of the Lord.

Because of this experience I know firsthand the danger of a whiteout. A whiteout is a weather condition in which visibility is severely reduced by snow. The horizon disappears completely, and there are no reference points at all, leaving the individual with a distorted orientation. That is what's happening today in the church. The reference points, the ancient landmarks, have been covered. In a whiteout no shadows are cast due to a continuous white cloud layer that appears to merge with the white snow surface.

If you find this hard to comprehend, I pray you will never experience this horrific phenomenon. I describe it as "white blindness." When it occurs, those caught within it are at the mercy of its power.

The vision revealed to me that layers upon layers of snow have been steadily covering the solid traditional truth of Christ. As with a whiteout, the truth has been lost in its flurry. This swirling, steady downfall of white powder can disorient the believer, blinding him as to which direction to go.

This chapter begins to follow the vision into the danger zone, where I will also offer some food for thought on many former and present-day whiteout conditions. You'll start to see that almost all doctrines that blow through the church have scriptural foundations. Some may be doctrines of devils. Others are teachings from well-intentioned leaders who broke away from their God-given moorings.

How does deception enter the church? How does false teaching infiltrate the body of Christ? It's obvious that no one who loves the Lord would willingly preach deception or error, and yet a spiritual whiteout of unhealthy, unbalanced, and, in some cases, downright unbiblical teaching has blinded the body of Christ in America, and it is quickly spreading around the world.

HOW HAS THIS HAPPENED?

There are different ways that unhealthy and destructive teaching can enter the church. Sometimes one biblical truth is taught to the exclusion of other biblical truths, thereby producing a dangerous imbalance. At other times one biblical truth is taught in an exaggerated way, often going beyond what Scripture actually says, and in the end does more harm than good. At other times clear biblical warnings are ignored or reinterpreted so radically that they lose all impact or effect, leaving people totally vulnerable and exposed.

Sadly, many sincere leaders have been misled, thereby misleading others and contributing to this whiteout of unhealthy, unbalanced, and even unbiblical teaching. They have preached one part of God's character while leaving out other parts of His character. They have taken one foundational scriptural truth and neglected other foundational scriptural truths. They have gotten so excited about one biblical revelation that they have presented it in an exaggerated, harmful way. In doing so, they have deceived themselves into thinking that the warnings of the Word no longer apply to them or their hearers.

"But," you ask, "how could this happen to mature spiritual leaders?"

Well, not all leaders in the body of Christ today are mature, and many do not have a solid foundation in the Word. Others are much more solid in their faith, but in their zeal to combat one error, they go to such an extreme that they end up in error themselves. Others have been transformed by the discovery of a biblical truth to the point that they start reading (and reinterpreting) the Word in light of that one truth, causing distortion of the biblical message. Others simply fail to realize that their flesh is subconsciously looking for a way to avoid the cross, leading to all kinds of false teaching.

From this point on I will be giving you many scripture references rather than printing out entire chapters. Something powerful happens when we personally search the scriptures. I believe the Holy Spirit will plant the seed of truth so deep in your heart that nothing will be able to uproot it. Also, when you see references to 1 and 2 Timothy, there is a deep purpose to placing these texts before you. During my years with Leonard Ravenhill, he required me to read 1 and 2 Timothy. He said, "Read them every day for a month, outside of your regular devotions. After a month take some time off, then read them again, every day for another month. They will revolutionize your life." He was right.

Of course, every Christian group feels like it has the whole message—or the right message—but Scripture gives us ways to test the message to see if it is really from the Lord. Consider Paul's words to Timothy: "All Scripture is God-breathed and is useful for teaching, rebuking, correcting and training in righteousness, so that the man of God may be thoroughly equipped for every good work" (2 Tim. 3:16–17, NIV).

Did you catch that? God's inspired Word is not just for encouragement and edification. It is for "teaching, rebuking, correcting and training in righteousness." Is that part of your scriptural diet? Are your leaders challenging you to go deeper in God? Are they speaking loving words of rebuke and correction when needed? Are they training you in righteousness along with teaching you "positive" truths?

Paul urged Timothy to "correct, rebuke and encourage—with great patience and careful instruction" (2 Tim. 4:2, NIV). There you have it again. Paul didn't tell Timothy to "encourage, encourage, encourage" but to "correct, rebuke and encourage." If that is not part of our spiritual diet, then we will be spiritually unhealthy and unbalanced.

And Paul added a warning of his own: "The time will come when they will not endure sound doctrine, but according to their own desires, because they have itching ears, they will heap up for themselves teachers; and they will turn their ears away from the truth, and be turned aside to fables" (vv. 3–4).

> **We must remember that Jesus came in grace and truth, not grace and grace.**

This is another way we can test the message: Does it always tell me what my itching ears want to hear, or does it rebuke my flesh? Does it give me a way to avoid the cross, or does it call me to pick up my cross daily? Does it allow me to cater to my sinful desires, or does it call me to die to sinful desires?

We must remember that Jesus came in grace and truth (John 1:14, 17), not grace and grace. Is that the message we are living and preaching?

At a tearful, emotional meeting in Miletus Paul told the elders of Ephesus that he would never see them again. With deep conviction he said to them, "Therefore I testify to you this day that I am innocent of the blood of all men. For I have not shunned to declare to you the whole counsel of God" (Acts 20:26–27). Can we say this today as leaders in the body? Can we say to our congregants and hearers, "I haven't shied away from declaring to you the whole message of God"?

When Paul said to Timothy that "all Scripture is God-breathed," he was speaking of the Old Testament, the only Scripture the first believers had. And he was referring to the Old Testament when he said that it was "useful for teaching, rebuking, correcting and training in righteousness, so that the man of God may be thoroughly equipped for every good work" (2 Tim. 3:16–17, NIV). That tells us that anyone who denigrates the Old Testament or makes it irrelevant for believers today is not preaching "the whole counsel of God." My last sermon at the Brownsville Revival was entitled, "Cry Wolf." I was warning the congregation of the dangers to come. This scripture was heavy on my heart and tears flowed throughout as I preached the message. For five years, to more than four million people, I had not ever refrained from preaching the whole counsel of God.

There are others today who claim that the message of Jesus was for Jews living before the cross. Since the cross, they claim, it is the teachings of Paul that we must follow rather than the teachings of Jesus (as if there were a contradiction between the two). As crazy as that sounds, it is catching on in certain circles today. After all, the teachings of Jesus are radical and challenging. Maybe there's a way we can avoid them!

Obviously anyone who leaves out the teachings of Jesus or denies their relevance for believers today cannot possibly be preaching "the whole counsel of God." And what do these people do with the words of Jesus in the Book of Revelation, warning the churches in Asia Minor? Do they dismiss those too? Some of them do!

FALSE TEACHING

Let me give you some concrete examples of how false teaching enters the body and then how this false teaching turns into a whiteout of error.

The carnal prosperity message

How did this message enter the church? There's no question that some adherents of the carnal prosperity message are motivated by greed, as were the false prophets of ancient Israel and the early church. (See Jeremiah 6:11–14; Jude 11.) For them, preaching Jesus is a means of financial gain, something that Paul rebuked in the strongest possible terms, speaking of men "of corrupt minds and destitute of the truth, who suppose that godliness is a means of gain" (1 Tim. 6:5).

Yet there are many sincere believers who have embraced this message, and they have lots of scriptures to back their case. They can point to godly people like Abraham and Job who were wealthy as a direct result of God's blessing (Gen. 13:2; Job 1:1–3). They can point to the covenant blessings the Lord promised to Israel for their obedience, blessings that explicitly included financial prosperity. (See Deuteronomy 28:1–13.)

In contrast, they can point out that the covenantal curses included poverty. (See Deuteronomy 28:14–68.) And they would be quick to remind us of very clear passages like Deuteronomy 8:18, which told the Israelites that it was God "who gives you power to get wealth, that He may establish His covenant."

They could also point to many verses in Proverbs and the Psalms that link financial prosperity to generosity, hard work, godly living, and faith. (See Psalm 112.) And they could remind us of wonderful promises like Proverbs 3:9–10. Then turning to the New Testament, they could demonstrate how Jesus reiterated these same promises with teachings like, "Give, and it will be given to you" (Luke 6:38). And they could also quote Paul, who wrote about the financial principles of sowing and reaping. (See 1 Corinthians 9; 2 Corinthians 8–9; Philippians 4:11–19.)

Are you with me? I am not against you having money. But I am adamantly against money having you.

Some will argue that the Bible consistently teaches that "the blessing of the LORD makes one rich, and He adds no sorrow with it" (Prov. 10:22).

The problem is, there's more to the story that the carnal prosperity preachers fail to mention:

1. Jesus warned against storing up treasures on earth (Matt. 6:19–24).

2. He warned against covetousness (Luke 12:15).

3. Jesus emphasized caring for the poor (Matt. 25:31–46).

4. Paul and John both taught that we should not live according to this present age (1 Cor. 7:29–31; 1 John 2:15–17).

5. Jesus did not die to make us financially wealthy but to save us from our sins (Matt. 1:21).

6. God chose the poor to be rich in faith and to be kingdom heirs (James 2:5).

More importantly, the carnal prosperity preachers have ignored other biblical warnings, like Paul's powerful words to Timothy:

> Those who desire to be rich fall into temptation and a snare, and into many foolish and harmful lusts which drown men in destruction and perdition. For the love of money is a root of all kinds of evil, for which some have strayed from the faith in their greediness, and pierced themselves through with many sorrows. But you, O man of God, flee these things and pursue righteousness, godliness, faith, love, patience, gentleness.
> —1 TIMOTHY 6:9–11

In stark contrast, carnal prosperity preachers encourage God's people to seek after riches—or to seek after God for the purpose of riches—often even judging your spirituality by the kind of car you drive. What in the world does that have to do with the gospel of Jesus?

Have you ever tested the control of money or material possessions in your life? Jeri and I have. We've given away our only car, donated money until it hurt, and shared with others material items that we loved. This is not boasting by any means. It's always been a personal inventory of what was the most important thing in our lives.

The hyper-grace message

Just like some carnal prosperity preachers are motivated by greed, some hyper-grace preachers are motivated by license to sin. The word *hyper* is actually a prefix that means "excess" or "exaggeration." When I use the term *hyper-grace*, I'm saying that by exaggerating God's amazing grace, we are actually diminishing this incredible trait of Jesus. His grace, or undeserved favor toward us, should be so overwhelming that we choose to do everything He requires and more. Jesus said, "If you love Me, you'll obey Me." I'll take that one step further: "If you appreciate My grace, live a godly life." We make Him happy when we live a holy life.

Think about a father and mother who work endlessly to provide for their child. How painful it is when that child takes advantage of that love. Rather than honoring his father and mother, he dishonors them by stealing or living in a way that breaks their hearts.

This exaggerated teaching of grace has become an epidemic. In our travels we are finding how widespread this heresy is. It has slipped in almost unnoticed and taken root like an unwanted weed—easy to get in but very hard to get out of the Christian. I have personally dealt with many young people who were once on fire but fell under this "kicked-back" view of God. Now, instead of pursuing Him, they are partying. This "unmerited freedom," if not tackled and taken out, will spread to future generations, and we will be left with millions of lukewarm Christians who have traded their passion for poison.

But, sadly, some hyper-grace preachers are living in sin and are looking for a way to ease their consciences, so they preach about a God who is all love and who never condemns, a God who doesn't judge us by our conduct. This is similar to the false teachers Jude confronted, stating that they "turn the grace of our God into lewdness" (Jude 4). The New International Version describes *lewdness* in this verse as "a license for immorality."

But there are plenty of hyper-grace preachers who truly love Jesus and are not looking for a way to justify sin, yet they are preaching truth mixed with error. Once again they have taken undeniable, glorious truths about God—this time about His grace—and presented them in such an exaggerated form that they nullify all divine warnings and even go as far as to claim that the words of Jesus do not apply to new covenant believers.

They rightly emphasize that we are saved by grace and not by works (Eph. 2:8–9), that while we were yet sinners Christ died for us (Rom. 5:6–8), that we are no longer sinners but saints in God's sight (1 Cor. 1:2), that God's love for us is not based on our performance (Rom. 5:9–10), that having begun in the Spirit we cannot become perfect by human effort (Gal. 3:3), that we are now sons and daughters of God, joint heirs with Jesus (Rom. 8:15–17), and more!

But they ignore mountains of other scriptural truths, also drawing wrong theological conclusions. For example, they rightly teach that Jesus died for all our sins—past, present, and future—but they wrongly conclude that as believers we no longer have to deal with sin (meaning we never have to confess sin or repent of sin, and the Holy Spirit no longer convicts us of sin).

There is not a drop of exaggeration or a bit of embellishment in these writings. Space does not permit me to share the hundreds of stories that flooded my life from shipwrecked believers who have fallen into this avalanche terrain. They had been deceived and were now at the point of dying. By the true grace of God we were able to rescue them from the near-fatal consequences of these teachings.

What then do they do with the verses that speak of us repenting of our sins or confessing our sins to God? They change the meaning of repentance (saying it only refers to a change of mind, and so repentance simply means to agree with God), and they claim that the call to confess our sins in 1 John applies only to unbelievers.

> **You know there is danger when the words of Jesus are willfully ignored.**

And what do the hyper-grace teachers do with the fact that Jesus, speaking by the Spirit, convicted believers of their sins (Rev. 2–3)? They either ignore the verses entirely or they claim, somehow, that the verses can't apply to us today. When I asked one hyper-grace proponent what he did with these messages of Jesus to the seven churches of Asia Minor in Revelation 2 and 3, he said to me, "If you base your theology on the Book of Revelation, you'll end up in a mess!"

You know there is danger when the words of Jesus are willfully ignored.

Antinomianism

It's a short jump from the hyper-grace message to complete antinomianism, which literally means "against law." In practice it means that "anything goes," since Jesus has set us free. "You're not going to put me into bondage," the antinomians say to us. "I'm not falling into your religious trap. Jesus set me free!" The problem is, Jesus didn't set us free to sin; He set us free from sin.

Once again there are scriptural truths that antinomians emphasize, such as we are under grace, not law (Rom. 6:14); we died to the law so that we could now live to serve God (Rom. 7:1–6); and we are no longer under the tutelage of the law (Gal. 3:24–25).

> **Jesus didn't set us free *to* sin;**
> **He set us free *from* sin.**

What they fail to realize is that now, under the new covenant, the law is written on our hearts (Heb. 8:10), and Jesus died for us and broke the power of sin on our lives so that now, by the Spirit, we can live out the righteous requirements of the law (Rom. 8:1–4).

And they fail to realize that Jesus calls us beyond the requirements of the law in His teaching, stating, for example, that adultery refers to adultery of the heart and not just the physical act (Matt. 5:27–28).

As for the law itself, Paul wrote that "the law is holy, and the commandment holy and just and good" (Rom. 7:12), and so God's perfect, holy, glorious law is not the problem. Sinful flesh is the problem, and once we have died to the flesh, it becomes our nature to be holy, just as the Lord is holy (1 Pet. 1:14–16).

If we choose to live in this "freedom to sin," then we need to know the "fate on the other end." Do you know anyone who has backslidden? Did it surprise you? They were once on fire for God but are now as cold as ice. Here's the truth.

Sin will take hold of your hand, kiss you on the cheek, whisper empty promises into your love-struck ear, woo you into the bed-chamber, lull you to sleep, and then stab you in the back.

Sin will take you farther than you ever wanted to go. Sin will cost you more than you ever wanted to pay. And sin will keep you longer than you ever intended to stay. Sin will promise you everything but leave you with nothing. Sin will love you for a season and curse you for eternity.

For all the antinomians out there who believe "anything goes," the question is, where do you end up?

Deification of man

We should be well aware that Satan is an incredible promoter. He is thrilled when man is lifted up to the place of God. Remember, when he was Lucifer in heaven, he practiced self-deification. He said, "I will ascend above the heights of the clouds, I will be like the Most High" (Isa. 14:14). This same spirit has permeated our society, both religious and secular.

Many false teachings today have this in common: they start with man rather than with God. In contrast, when Paul laid out the gospel message in Romans, he started with God and then went to man: He is holy and we are not; He is righteous and we are not; we are under His judgment and in need of mercy, and that mercy comes through the cross.

Today's gospel, especially in America, has a very different ring to it: rather than being all about God, it's all about me. In fact, just as the American way is to make everything bigger and better, the

American gospel basically says that Jesus came to make you into a bigger and better you. That is not the gospel!

> Jesus said to His disciples, "If anyone desires to come after Me, let him deny himself, and take up his cross, and follow Me. For whoever desires to save his life will lose it, but whoever loses his life for My sake will find it."
>
> —MATTHEW 16:24–25

> And He…said to them, "If anyone comes to Me and does not hate his father and mother, wife and children, brothers and sisters, yes, and his own life also, he cannot be My disciple. And whoever does not bear his cross and come after Me cannot be My disciple."
>
> —LUKE 14:25–27

> Jesus answered them… "Most assuredly, I say to you, unless a grain of wheat falls into the ground and dies, it remains alone; but if it dies, it produces much grain. He who loves his life will lose it, and he who hates his life in this world will keep it for eternal life."
>
> —JOHN 12:23–25

How different this is from the man-centered all-about-me gospel message of today!

My friend, I was raised totally different. When you became a Christian, you went down the ladder rather than up the ladder. There was no rising to the place of hierarchy. I was instructed to lower myself to the place of humility. My heart is overwhelmed with appreciation for God placing me around men and women of God who never lifted themselves up. Christ was the King, and we all lived to serve Him. There was a song that had a phrase something like this, "If you want to be great in God's kingdom, learn to be the servant of all."

My heart is broken over the arrogance of many of today's ministers. During a television program a few months ago I looked into the camera and asked the viewing audience to forgive us. I said that I was representing all the ministers of the world. I begged all the viewers to pardon the arrogance, the excessive fund-raising, the lies, the manipulation, the false prophecy. I was crying out as a representative of the clergy to please forgive. The bottom line? Many preachers of today, as they continue on in their charlatan ways, deserve to be looked upon as con artists. Where is the brokenness? Where is the deep humility? Where are the tears? Where is the passion for souls? Can anyone find Jesus in this parade of self-promoted piety?

> **Just as the American way is to make everything bigger and better, the American gospel basically says that Jesus came to make you into a bigger and better you.**

Before moving on to our next layer of snow, let me take you back to one of my dear mentors in the Lord. His name is Jim Summers. We were on a farm shoveling cow manure. He was our spiritual leader. He walked up wearing a suit. He jumped on the back of the truck, grabbed a shovel, and began unloading this truckload of stenchy filth. I looked at him in amazement. He was preaching one minute and shoveling dung the next. These are the kind of leaders I was raised around. They wouldn't dare let us deify man. Jesus was everything.

We are in grave danger worldwide as millions upon millions gaze upon man rather than gaze upon God. It is a setup for the Antichrist; as we become so accustomed to worshipping man, it will be a simple maneuver for the Antichrist to move into position.

This is what will happen when man, not the Lord, comes first, when the teaching of the gospel revolves around God serving us rather than us serving Him.

Challenging the authority of the Word

This lie goes back to the Garden of Eden, beginning with the serpent's challenge to Eve: "Has God indeed said, 'You shall not eat of every tree of the garden'?" (Gen. 3:1). Are you sure He really meant that? Are you sure you are not putting your own interpretation on it? And are you sure it's really God's Word at all?

Perhaps people just made it up. Perhaps these are just human traditions that religious leaders concocted to keep you under their power.

The satanic challenge in the garden was twofold: First, did God really say that? And second, God didn't really mean what He said. After all, you won't die if you eat from the tree (Gen. 3:1–5).

That twofold challenge continues to assault us today. First, best-selling authors tell us that the biblical text is not reliable, that the biblical manuscripts we have in our possession are hopelessly contradictory, and that we can know little or nothing about the real, historical Jesus. Then other best-selling authors tell us that the Bible is no more than a collection of religious traditions and that God Himself is nothing more than a religious myth. In other words, "You won't die if you disregard the Scriptures and disobey what is written. God isn't even there."

For the most part, though, the challenge to the authority of the Scriptures is subtler, and some of it flows out of the deification of man: "The Bible must live up to my standards. I will judge the God of the Bible based on my morality rather than the God of the Bible judging me based on His morality."

Because of this mentality it is more and more common to hear believers talk about the problem they have with the God of the Old Testament or to question whether the Bible really means what it says, a case in point being a pro-homosexual reading of Scripture. The problem is not that the verses aren't clear. The problem is that we know homosexuals who say they really love the Lord and seem to be very Christlike, and they are devoted to each other as a couple and even pray together in the Spirit.

> **When the Scriptures contradict our feelings and preferences, rather than crucify our feelings and preferences and bow down before God and His Word, we question God's Word.**

So what do we do? Rather than say to the practicing homosexuals, "You may be very sincere, but the Word of God is very clear," we question what the Word says despite its clarity. And so, rather than speaking the truth in love to sinners and telling them that if they want to please the Lord and be in right relationship with Him, they must take up the cross and follow Him, we reinterpret (or rewrite) the Word.

In short, when the Scriptures contradict our feelings and preferences, rather than crucify our feelings and preferences and bow down before God and His Word, we question God's Word.

There is no future punishment

Nowhere is this questioning of God's Word seen any more clearly than when it comes to the subject of hell and future punishment. And because we preach an imbalanced gospel—emphasizing God's love and ignoring His wrath, emphasizing His mercy and ignoring His justice—we no longer have room for hell and future punishment in our theology.

After all, if we can reject the God of the Old Testament because He ordered the children of Israel to exterminate the Canaanites, we can reject the God of the New Testament because He will one day cast sinners into hell.

And if we're not willing to reject this God entirely, what do we do? We rewrite the troublesome verses, saying things like, "Hell is here and now." Or, "When Jesus talked about hell, He was talking about a garbage dump outside of Jerusalem. It was only a figure of speech."

Then why did Jesus use such strong language in talking about the fire of hell and about people weeping and wailing and gnashing their teeth (e.g., Matt. 8:12)? And why did He teach that "it is more profitable for you that one of your members perish, than for your whole body to be cast into hell" (Matt. 5:29)? And why do other New Testament writers warn us repeatedly about the wrath to come (e.g., Eph. 5:1–6)?

It's one thing to debate the exact nature of the future punishment that awaits those who reject the gospel. It's another thing to downplay or eliminate it. As the writer of Hebrews warned, "It is a fearful thing to fall into the hands of the living God" (Heb. 10:31). Whatever legitimate debate we may have on the precise nature of the coming judgment, this much is clear from the Word: it will be irreversible, dreadful, and of eternal consequence.

Why, then, aren't we warning the lost to flee from the coming wrath and run into the loving arms of the Savior?

I can hear the words of Leonard Ravenhill. He would say, "Steve, there are judgments to come for everyone. The Bible says that we have an appointment to die, and after that the judgment [Heb 9:27]. For the Christian, one day you will be judged for everything you did while here on earth [1 Cor 3:13], and His judgment will be by fire. Make sure, on that day, you are not standing knee deep in ashes."

And let's not forget the future punishment of those who choose to not believe. Perhaps you are one of those who never had the opportunity to hear about the judgments. Therefore you haven't had the freedom to make up your own mind. The Word is clear and not subject to every man's interpretation. I remember this from my early days: "the Bible says it, I believe it, and that settles it." WRONG! The Bible says it, and that settles it whether I believe it or not.

Revelation 20:11–15 clearly warns about the coming Great White Throne Judgment. Yet modern-day heresy teachers have taken upon themselves the authority to erase the judgment. They have chosen to drop dangerous layers of snow on top of the other damning layers. The result, if believed and followed, will be too devastating to mention. I cannot begin to imagine the surprise on people's faces as they stand before the King of kings and the Lord of lords.

Universal reconciliation

There is one last step to take, and that is the step of universal reconciliation, the teaching that in the end everyone will make it into heaven because of Jesus' death on the cross. (Note: Some people think universal reconciliation and universalism are one and the same, but they are not. In contrast, universalism teaches that all paths, all religions, lead to God.) There may be some future suffering, but it will be purging rather than punishment, and ultimately everyone will be saved.

Proponents of universal reconciliation point to verses that teach that God reconciled to Himself "all things to Himself, by Him, whether things on earth or things in heaven, having made peace through the blood of His cross" (Col. 1:20). And they point out that just as in Adam all die, in Jesus all will live (Rom. 5:12–21).

At the same time they must ignore all the verses—and there are many—that state clearly that there will be a final separation between the saved and the lost, a separation that is forever (e.g., Dan. 12:2; Matt. 13:41–43; 25:46; John 5:28–29; Rom. 2:6–11; 2 Thess. 1:5–10). They are like the false prophets of Israel who told the people all is well when nothing was well, superficially treating their wound rather than healing it (Jer. 6:14).

And when they do try to interact with the verses that speak of eternal punishment, like Matthew 25:46, they come up with impossible interpretations like, "The word for 'punishment' actually means purging. It speaks of a future purging for the purpose of salvation, not a future punishment as a final penalty for sin."

So this is where we find ourselves today: a gentle breeze of false teaching has become a strong wind of serious error, some of it downright heretical, and a storm of doctrinal deviation has become a massive deadly whiteout.

You have been presented with many layers of snow that have made up the spiritual avalanche. This threat of false teaching could kill millions. But it is not going to be you!

In the next chapter we'll take a look at what happens in the natural when a life-threatening avalanche is imminent, and I'll provide you with an understanding of what you need to do to destroy this deadly threat before it destroys you. Look out!

Chapter 8

FIRE on the MOUNTAIN

AFTER RECEIVING THIS VISION, I PURSUED ACCURATE avalanche information from those who would know best. There were too many daunting details, so livid, so exact, that my natural man immediately put my spiritual man in check. I was to examine every portion of what had been received.

The process of self-examination was ingrained in my spirit at Bible school by David Wilkerson. Some readers may be unfamiliar with this man of God and his decades of influence throughout the world. He is best known for working with the street-hardened gangs of New York City and was later memorialized in the book and movie *The Cross and the Switchblade*. I mention him often, as his was the most powerful voice speaking into my life as a young evangelist.

Reverend Wilkerson referred to my wife and me as his son and daughter in the faith, an honor that I felt we never deserved but humbly accepted. Of course, due to the nature of his work, the international drug rehab program Teen Challenge, he had thousands of spiritual children.

Brother Dave, as we all called him, often warned his students of the pitfalls and dangers of spiritual revelations. Upon receiving a word from the Lord, we were responsible to intensely scrutinize every detail under the biblical microscope of God's Word. If it didn't line up with the Holy Bible, then it wasn't from God. Period!

And rightly so. Why should anyone believe me? Who am I to be delivering a message from the Most High God? I'm just a drug addict saved by grace. How do I know my dream or vision isn't actually just an LSD flashback?

Don't be afraid if the Lord gives you a fresh prophecy. After all, you are all to pursue that gift, as Paul said, "Pursue love, and desire spiritual gifts, but especially that you may prophesy" (1 Cor. 14:1). However, you are responsible to test everything you do: "But let each one examine his own work, and then he will have rejoicing in himself alone, and not in another. For each one shall bear his own load" (Gal. 6:4–5). How true and sobering are those words! And then, "Examine yourselves as to whether you are in the faith. Test yourselves. Do you not know yourselves, that Jesus Christ is in you?—unless indeed you are disqualified" (2 Cor. 13:5). How do you test yourself? By making sure what you say and do are in line with the Bible. If everyone would follow these biblical mandates, it would keep us all on track and ensure that we maintain accuracy in our words.

I feel I must add the counsel of another spiritual giant that I mention often in my sermons and writings. Leonard Ravenhill constantly spoke of receiving words from God and warned us of the dangers of young, immature spiritual cadets stealing His glory. I can see that eighty-year-old seasoned warrior pointing his finger at you and me and belting out, "Never be found guilty of taking a drop of God's deserved glory. Take no credit for your successes. If it wasn't for Jesus, you wouldn't have the breath to breathe. God gets all the glory!"

So with this vision freshly imparted, it was time for a spiritual dissection. A quick phone call to a friend living in the Colorado Rockies put me in contact with someone "high up" in the ski patrol. I was shocked when he called only an hour after being notified. Without hesitation I shared the entire vision. I knew there was a possibility of him regarding me as a spiritual kook, but it was worth the chance.

The opposite was true. He treated me as a fellow comrade in the fight for people's lives. The officer confirmed what I saw in the vision concerning the destruction of avalanches. He said that the bombs, helicopters, and heavy artillery that I saw are all used to defuse the danger. He said, "At the sign of danger, I personally man an anti-tank artillery weapon with 105mm howitzer shells. The cannon is set on the base highway, aimed at the mountain, and I begin firing. Some of the explosives set off avalanches five miles away." (More will be learned of his work in chapter 9, "Hell on the Highway.")

Then the officer began to startle me with information. He spoke about the dangers of winter sports, especially backcountry skiing. His serious tone of voice seemed to be that of a military watchman. His responsibility was the same as mine: life and death. He wasn't in this vital position to make friends. On the contrary, due to his often direct, unwanted warnings he would cause the recipients to "attack back." Without wavering, he would scream at arrogant professional skiers as they mounted their snowmobiles hoping to catch some white powder in the backcountry. He would ardently shout out his professional opinion, always willing to catch flak from those who felt superior and invincible.

A loving father screams out to his little boy to look both ways before crossing the street. These loving rangers scream out to grown boys and girls to look both ways before launching themselves down the mountain. The little boy who pays no attention is hit by a distracted driver. The skiers who pay no attention are hit by a wave of unforgiving snow.

This reminds me of the work of the ministry. A man or woman called of God will preach, warn, exhort, and oftentimes passionately prepare a message that will infuriate some and offend others. Thankfully there are always those who are saved because they choose to listen and obey.

I've been delivering God's Word for many decades. My goal has never been to make more friends. Most of us need to reduce our friendship circle and surround ourselves with those who are truly committed.

What motivates you as a Christian to wake up every day? According to the Word of God we should be consumed with populating heaven: "For this is good and acceptable in the sight of God our Savior, who desires all men to be saved and to come to the knowledge of the truth" (1 Tim. 2:3–4). Jesus wants everyone to repent and make it to heaven: "The Lord is not slack concerning His promise, as some count slackness, but is longsuffering toward us, not willing that any should perish but that all should come to repentance" (2 Pet. 3:9).

Do we want more friends around our table down here or want to fill up His table up there? I recently shared the gospel with a waiter who was completely uninterested but obviously affected by my presentation. It was direct, in love, and came with an invitation that penetrated his heart. When I said that I wanted him in heaven with me, there was a change in his countenance. He said he didn't want Jesus right now but that he wanted to learn more by visiting our Internet sites. "I'm going to do this," he said, "because of how you presented God to me."

You see, as Christians our responsibility is identical to those mountain rangers. They must warn of impending danger. What people do with it is up to them. We are responsible for our actions, not theirs.

I love the Word. When you see scriptures woven in and out of my writings, please take time to absorb them. Even familiar texts should be given special attention. When we grow weary of His Word, we are growing weary of Him. He says, "We must all appear before the judgment seat of Christ, that each one may receive the things done in the body, according to what he has done, whether good or bad. Knowing, therefore, the terror of the Lord, we persuade men" (2 Cor. 5:10–11).

Jesus said, "I say to you that for every idle word men may speak, they will give account of it in the day of judgment. For by your words you will be justified, and by your words you will be condemned" (Matt. 12:36–37).

Oftentimes the unheeded cries of the ski patrol end in tragedy. After the avalanche comes, it is too late. Protocol demands a sled full of body bags and a sobering ride to the danger zone. Manned with avalanche probes, professional snow shovels, and electronic detectors, the team races to the ravines hoping to locate these precious people. Paramedics are onboard for those who might have survived, but the chances are slim. Within a few minutes an avalanche, like a killer on a mission, buries the skier. Oxygen is in short supply. Most die from suffocation.

I learned that an avalanche can reach speeds of 150 miles per hour within a minute.[1] I could not comprehend that velocity. I had driven on the autobahn in Germany in a rental car that began to violently shake at those speeds. The fear was overwhelming. I felt as if the well-built machine that I was driving was about to disintegrate.

Once an avalanche fractures, or breaks apart, and begins to take on speed, it can reach sixty to eighty miles per hour within five seconds.[2] Five seconds? That's insane. Who could escape a torrential slide of that magnitude? I've learned that the speed depends on various factors, such as the temperature, consistency of the snow, the wind, and freedom from obstacles. Regardless, while running its course, the avalanche will mow down everything and everyone in its path.

How could snow pick up that kind of speed? Once again I thought of the helplessness of believers who are in the avalanche path of false teaching. They would be picked up, carried downhill, smothered, and killed in an instant!

READY, AIM, FIRE!

In this chapter I am speaking of weapon fire—actually firing on the mountain with the intent of destroying it before it destroys us. As Christians we are to aim our weapons at the deluge of deceptive teaching. We are to bring it down before it comes down on its own, releasing its fury on the innocent followers of Jesus. We are to aim our spiritual military weaponry at the hillside, hoping to dislodge the snow while skiers sleep.

I have learned valuable eternal lessons from those rangers and their writings that will forever remain part of my obligations to God. I have learned of the inherent risk of targeting avalanche terrain. The ones who are willing to do anything to prevent death by avalanche could actually be putting themselves in harm's way. These sliding killers are no respecter of persons.

I am shaking and weeping as a spiritual analogy just swept through my heart. I know how Satan comes to steal, kill, and destroy. He often attacks while Christians are at their lowest spiritually. Their lamps are void of oil, their joy has been stolen, and their strength has been depleted.

I have committed myself to joining ranks with Jesus to destroy the works of the devil because "he who sins is of the devil, for the devil has sinned from the beginning. For this purpose the Son of God was manifested, that He might destroy the works of the devil" (1 John 3:8).

Becoming casual creates casualties.

Now with this avalanche hovering over the church, I see no other design but for it to steal precious truths from young lives. The innocent will wander into its path and believe the lies. The destruction that comes is well documented in the natural and is now, sadly, becoming documented in the spiritual. People who were once on fire for God have had their flame smothered, their genuine zeal replaced by carnal excitement, their hopes and dreams of doing great things for God replaced by the spirit of the age of eat, drink, and be merry. As Jesus warned:

> As it was in the days of Noah, so it will be also in the days of the Son of Man: They ate, they drank, they married wives, they were given in marriage, until the day that Noah entered the ark, and the flood came and destroyed them all. Likewise as it was also in the days of Lot: They ate, they drank, they bought, they sold, they planted, they built; but on the day that Lot went out of Sodom it rained fire and brimstone from heaven and destroyed them all. Even so will it be in the day when the Son of Man is revealed.
> —Luke 17:26–30

While discussing with the avalanche patrol the dangers of what lay ahead, I became more determined than ever to involve myself in this violent war. Of course, mine is spiritual, but the cost of life is strikingly similar. The ski patrols, who operate worldwide, are devoted to melting and mutilating mountains of unwanted snow with powerful explosives.

I'm asking all Christians and spiritual leaders to take care and observe all safety precautions. People die when they begin to treat dangerous terrain as common. Becoming casual creates casualties.

Right now, throughout the world, due to the accelerated increase of false teaching, the likelihood of avalanches is certain. Ask yourself these questions before venturing out into unknown spiritual terrain:

1. Do you have the skill, knowledge, and training to detect a potential threatening condition?

2. Can you rescue yourself should someone come along with a convincing argument? Do you have the right questions? Do you have a plan?

3. Have you checked the current spiritual weather condition of that particular ministry? Are they forecasting truth? Or do you sense a possibility of false reporting? Are you shunned when you detect the hint of error and mention it to the leadership?

4. Have you checked with other spiritual friends who aren't afraid of sharing exactly what they feel?

5. Do you have an escape route for those caught, should this present teaching, or lack thereof, be erroneous?

6. Lastly, have you isolated yourself from others who once walked in freedom with you? Are you skiing (spiritually) alone?

Many bodies are found in areas that are closed by patrols. Isolating ourselves is always dangerous. Accountability brings stability.

These avalanches must be destroyed *before* the believer flies into their path.

LET'S REVISIT THE VISION

I think it is important for us to revisit the vision throughout this book. Why? Because it was given from God to us as a warning. This cannot become just a story, a spiritually educational e-book. So let's take a moment to remember what I saw.

The ski patrol operated like a well-trained platoon. Some boarded helicopters manned with small bombs; others jumped on snowmobiles loaded with handheld explosive devices. What seemed to be a strategic group of sharpshooters stationed at the base were maneuvering antitank weapons aimed at the snow-covered peaks. They fired their weapons at strategic points in the avalanche zone to force avalanches before the snow accumulated to a life-threatening depth. Left unchecked, the accumulation of heavy, dense snow packed on top of lighter snow could easily slide down with incredible speed and force, resulting in enormous damage and loss of life.

Just as the ski patrol did in this vision, those who are aware of what's happening in the church must take swift and accurate action. Their weapons of warfare must be aimed at the "peaks and avalanche terrain" to dispel the lies. Apostles, prophets, evangelists, pastors, and teachers must be willing to drop spiritual bombs, fire anti-heresy missiles, and even drive into the danger zones, armed with explosive truth to confront this potential avalanche. The generals of this generation must leave the war room and put their years of experience on the front lines.

As a potential officer enlisted to fire on the mountain, you must be equipped. Of course, fasting, prayer, and intense intercession will defuse much of the unseen spiritual element.

As Paul tells us, our weapons are spiritual:

> Finally, my brethren, be strong in the Lord and in the power of His might. Put on the whole armor of God, that you may be able to stand against the wiles of the devil. For we do not wrestle against flesh and blood, but against principalities, against powers, against the rulers of the darkness of this age, against spiritual hosts of wickedness in the heavenly places. Therefore take up the whole armor of God, that you may be able to withstand in the evil day, and having done all, to stand. Stand therefore, having girded your waist with truth, having put on the breastplate of righteousness, and having shod your feet with the preparation of the gospel of peace; above all, taking the shield of faith with which you will be able to quench all the fiery darts of the wicked one. And take the helmet of salvation, and the sword of the Spirit, which is the word of God; praying always with all prayer and supplication in the Spirit, being watchful to this end with all perseverance and supplication for all the saints.
> —Ephesians 6:10–18

The ski patrol, operating like a fine-tuned machine, uses three basic weapons: the helicopters dropping the bombs, the snowmobiles planting explosives in key avalanche terrain areas, and the antitank cannons launching shells up to five miles into the mountains. Using projectile explosives like the cannon is just one way that the ski patrol gets their firepower to the mountain peaks. Just as I saw in the vision, they deploy explosive charges on the peaks of the mountain range, even setting off larger charges on the slopes below. This was so incredibly interesting to me that I had to dig deeper into this dangerous profession to discover more. I found it fascinating and believe that many others will as well.

> **The generals of this generation must leave the war room and put their years of experience on the front lines.**

To combat deadly potential avalanches, the ski patrol employs an effective arsenal of weaponry. In the vision I saw military-style helicopters flying overhead manned with skilled professionals dropping bombs on the slopes below. Helicopters are fascinating; they instantly grab our attention when one passes overhead.

That is how the ski patrol reaches dangerous areas when other options are not available. Imagine flying over the beautiful white slopes of a tall mountain range. You're not sightseeing; your eyes are searching for the telltale signs of avalanches hiding below fresh-fallen snow. You're not in the pilot seat. You are the bombardier. It's your job to deploy explosive charges from the rear cabin where you are harnessed in at the open door. The pilot positions you just above a potential slide, allowing you to drop a charge with great accuracy onto the target zone below. You pull the igniter, ensure it is lit, and drop the charge.

"Shot away!"

"Shot away," the pilot confirms as he quickly maneuvers the helicopter to a safe position to view the results. The charge detonates and a small slide moves down the slope. The mission is a success, and the potentially deadly avalanche is destroyed.

When weather conditions, the dark of night, or other circumstances restrict the use of helicopters, the ski patrol must put their own lives in harm's way as they scale the steep slopes on foot or by snowmobile to deploy these charges. This is exactly what I saw in the vision. Individuals, operating like well-trained platoons mounting their snowmobiles, deploy to the mountainside to place controlled explosive charges on the mountain peaks above and the slopes below.

Don't take this lightly! These men and women place their lives on the line to combat these avalanches. Though every possible precaution is taken, the risk to their lives is never fully eliminated. Not long ago a veteran ski patrol officer was working with his team detonating these controlled explosions on a mountainside when the slope fractured beneath his feet, sweeping him down the mountain.[3] His team didn't find him in time. The very avalanche he sought to preempt ended his life.

I'm reminded how Jesus told His disciples, "I am the good shepherd. The good shepherd gives His life for the sheep. But a hireling, he who is not the shepherd, one who does not own the sheep, sees the wolf coming and leaves the sheep and flees; and the wolf catches the sheep and scatters them. The hireling flees because he is a hireling and does not care about the sheep. I am the good shepherd; and I know My sheep, and am known by My own. As the Father knows Me, even so I know the Father; and I lay down My life for the sheep" (John 10:11–15).

The most fascinating imagery I saw in the vision was that of the cannon used to blast the mountainside. I had no idea such tactics were used to combat an avalanche. Imagine my surprise as I found myself speaking with one of the officers who manned the cannon for the Colorado Ski Patrol. Picture these powerful cannons, strategically deployed along the base of the mountain. At the first sight of danger they are loaded with explosives, aimed at the tower peaks above, and fired. The sound is deafening, but the results save lives.

Just the other day I was purchasing a few groceries. As I checked out, I noticed the gentleman taking care of me had a crippled hand, and his body was noticeably disfigured. My assumption was that he was suffering from multiple sclerosis. A few seconds into our conversation I asked him if he knew Jesus as his personal Savior. He stopped what he was doing and looked me straight in the eyes and said, "God has watched over me all my life. My body was destroyed in Iraq. It was full of holes after two tours."

Our world is filled with hidden men and women like this hero. Without taking the opportunity to speak with him, I would have never known the value of this man's sacrifice. You might be surprised what you may learn with a little investigation. Out of respect to professionals and volunteers around the world who live and die protecting others, I dug deeper into the vision to better understand tools they use to wage warfare on the avalanches.

YOUR MOST POWERFUL WEAPON

Knowing what you believe is your most powerful weapon in combating false teaching. That's a simple but profound statement. Do you know what you believe? I urge you to always have scriptural projectiles ready to aim and fire at the first evidence of a spiritual avalanche.

Ready, aim, fire:

1. Man is a sinner.
"All have sinned and fall short of the glory of God" (Rom. 3:23).

2. Sin separates you from God.

"Your iniquities have separated you from your God, and your sins have hidden His face from you, so that He will not hear" (Isa. 59:2).

3. Sin will destroy you.

"The wages of sin is death, but the gift of God is eternal life in Christ Jesus our Lord" (Rom. 6:23).

4. Sin will enslave you.

"Jesus answered them, 'Most assuredly, I say to you, whoever commits sin is a slave of sin'" (John 8:34).

5. Sin will keep you from heaven.

"Do you not know that the unrighteous will not inherit the kingdom of God? Do not be deceived. Neither fornicators, nor idolaters, nor adulterers, nor homosexuals, nor sodomites, nor thieves, nor covetous, nor drunkards, nor revilers, nor extortioners will inherit the kingdom of God" (1 Cor. 6:9–10).

6. Without the shedding of blood there is no forgiveness of sin.

"And according to the law almost all things are purified with blood, and without shedding of blood there is no remission" (Heb. 9:22).

7. Jesus Christ shed His blood on Calvary, paying the full price for our sinful disobedience and opening the way for us to enter into fellowship with God.

"The next day John saw Jesus coming toward him, and said, 'Behold! The Lamb of God who takes away the sin of the world!'" (John 1:29).

"God demonstrates His own love toward us, in that while we were still sinners, Christ died for us" (Rom. 5:8).

For the snow enthusiasts that demand I put a positive scripture about snow, here it is: *"Come now, and let us reason together,"* says the Lord, *"Though your sins are like scarlet, they shall be as white as snow; though they are red like crimson, they shall be as wool"* (Isa. 1:18).

8. God wants everyone to be saved.

"The Lord is not slack concerning His promise, as some count slackness, but is longsuffering toward us, not willing that any should perish but that all should come to repentance" (2 Pet. 3:9).

9. We can be saved by faith in Jesus.

"If you confess with your mouth the Lord Jesus and believe in your heart that God has raised Him from the dead, you will be saved" (Rom. 10:9).

10. There is only one way to heaven.

"Jesus said to him, 'I am the way, the truth, and the life. No one comes to the Father except through Me'" (John 14:6).

11. Once you become a Christian, your lifestyle changes.

"If anyone is in Christ, he is a new creation; old things have passed away; behold, all things have become new" (2 Cor. 5:17).

These few spiritual truths have enough *dunamis* (dynamite) to blow up any heresy that comes your way. But you, my friend, must be convinced, committed, and living in covenant with your commander in chief, Jesus! At His command be ready to take aim without hesitation. Light the fuse! Pull the trigger! Fire on the mountain!

In the next chapter we'll discover that the avalanche's threat extended far beyond those who were gathered at the resort; just like in the vision, many people outside the walls of the church, and even believers around the world, are in danger.

....

NOTES

1. University of Nottingham, "Laboratory Avalanches Reveal Behaviour of Ice Flows," press release, December 14, 2011, http://www.nottingham.ac.uk/News/pressreleases/2011/december/laboratory-avalanches.aspx (accessed January 29, 2013).

2. National Geographic, "Avalanches," http://environment.nationalgeographic.com/environment/natural-disasters/avalanche-profile/ (accessed January 29, 2013).

3. Associated Press, "Veteran Alpine Meadows Ski Patrol Member Killed by Avalanche," December 25, 2012, http://sacramento.cbslocal.com/2012/12/25/alpine-meadows-ski-patrol-member-killed-in-avalanche/ (accessed January 29, 2013).

Chapter 9

HELL on the HIGHWAY

As you know by now, much research has gone into the details of what I saw in the vision. I have always been extremely dedicated to truth, whether we are talking about the eternal truth of the Bible or the simple day-to-day truth in conversation. Lies have always made me uncomfortable, and liars have always earned a place in my life as not worthy of attention. When I hear an evangelist stretch the truth or a pastor modify a story to better connect with his congregation, I cringe.

The worst liars are those who add to the Word of God with the intention of deceiving innocent hearers. The Word warns, "Every word of God is pure; He is a shield to those who put their trust in Him. Do not add to His words, lest He rebuke you, and you be found a liar" (Prov. 30:5–6), and of course we know where liars go. "But the cowardly, unbelieving, abominable, murderers, sexually immoral, sorcerers, idolaters, and all liars shall have their part in the lake which burns with fire and brimstone, which is the second death" (Rev. 21:8).

I say all that to help put you at peace as you read the words of this book. I take truth very seriously. The vision happened just the way you have read it, and the research has been sheer enjoyment. I have loved learning and relaying facts just as they were given to me.

As I mentioned in the last chapter, one of the first phone calls I made after the Lord spoke to me was to a friend who could connect me with the Colorado Ski Patrol. He confirmed what I saw concerning the avalanche as factual. The spiritual application was outside his realm of understanding. No problem. I knew what God was saying, and I had enough qualified theological friends to help me, should I need a deeper understanding of any portion of the vision.

When the ranger shared with me his assignment during avalanche warnings, I was intrigued. He operated the massive antitank weapon that produced enough power to launch a shell up to five miles.

My intense interest in his occupation actually comes from my heritage. I was born in Turkey. My father was a retired military officer under assignment to teach the Turkish army how to operate large tanks. During my childhood, stories would abound, hence my interest in tank weaponry.

I asked the ranger why shells were launched from such a long distance to reach potential disasters. He explained how these distant avalanche terrains were very remote but also dangerous. Many of these mountain peaks covered with layers of snow could give way at any moment, covering the roads below. These roads were heavily traveled by large trucks carrying supplies to the resorts, as well as by everyday motorists and vacationers who couldn't wait to arrive at their snowy paradise.

The mountains had to be swept clean of danger. The maneuvering, timing, and firing of this weapon were an exact science. The roads below had to be monitored, ensuring that no one would be killed. Occupants of the homes around the avalanche zone had to be notified that extreme explosives were going to be used to take control of this snowslide before it took on a killer life of its own.

There are people traveling down life's highway who are heading to Christendom, but false teaching will hit and kill their potential walk with God before they ever arrive.

Spiritual avalanches have the same MO (*modus operandi* or mode of operation) as avalanches in the natural. They leave death and destruction in their wake. By the time you conclude this book, I trust you will have gained the same understanding that thousands of others have attained. The layers of false teaching pose a serious threat to the furtherance of the pure gospel. This chapter is intended to let you know that we must not only destroy the avalanches hovering over the church but also look long range and destroy the distant avalanches that will kill many who have not yet reached the church where the pure gospel is being preached.

Let's make this just a bit clearer. There are people traveling down life's highway who are heading to Christendom, but false teaching will hit and kill their potential walk with God before they ever arrive. Someone will detour, discourage, and destroy their desires before they ever have the opportunity to hear the unadulterated truth.

KILLING MACHINES

Let me introduce you to some historical facts about avalanches that I hope will encourage you to become adamantly opposed to anything that resembles these demonic weapons of warfare.

Once again, avalanches are killing machines. I think you might even say they are serial killers. They have even played a deadly role in warfare throughout the ages. History records that military forces have used unsettled snow by triggering an avalanche and have watched as the white wave covered the unsuspecting enemy below.

Sounds like something the devil would do. I can see Satan waiting for a spiritual group of young people to come along and then opening fire, dumping every heretical lie he has. Of course, that's all he can do. There's no truth in him, as Jesus tells us: "You are of your father the devil, and the desires of your father you want to do. He was a murderer from the beginning, and does not stand in the truth, because there is no truth in him. When he speaks a lie, he speaks from his own resources, for he is a liar and the father of it" (John 8:44).

The apostle Paul repeatedly warned the new, innocent church of "layers of snow" hovering overhead: "But what I do, I will also continue to do, that I may cut off the opportunity from those who desire an opportunity to be regarded just as we are in the things of which they boast. For such are false apostles, deceitful workers, transforming themselves into apostles of Christ. And no wonder! For Satan himself transforms himself into an angel of light. Therefore it is no great thing if his ministers also transform themselves into ministers of righteousness, whose end will be according to their works" (2 Cor. 11:12–15).

Here are a few avalanche stories to better understand the danger. As I read these in relation to the vision, my resolve to fight becomes stronger and stronger.

- Not long ago 138 soldiers and civilians were buried in an avalanche in the mountains of Pakistan. It doesn't matter if you are armed with the latest military weaponry or how strong you feel your fortified position may be. You still are no match for the sheer force of a mighty avalanche.[1]

- They called it the Winter of Terror. The Swiss Alps were experiencing unusual weather patterns. Over a three-month period, a series of nearly 650 avalanches killed more than 265 people and destroyed many villages. One town was hit by six avalanches in one hour alone.[2]

- The worst military avalanche on record happened during World War I. Italian soldiers entrenched themselves in the highest peaks of the Alps. They dragged heavy weapons and artillery up the steep cliffs and built forts in the mountainside. The winter that year was especially harsh. The region had been blanketed with record amounts of snowfall. The heavy accumulation, combined with the explosive artillery power, caused massive avalanches that took out more than ten thousand troops. One military officer commented, "The mountains in winter are more dangerous than the Italians."[3]

But none of these compare to the story I'm about to share. It's a story I visualized so clearly as I read it that I could almost hear the people screaming. I think you'll understand its profound effect on me as you read on.

The Worst Avalanche in US History

The Wellington avalanche was the worst avalanche, measured in terms of lives lost, in the history of the United States. For around ten days in February of 1910, the small town of Wellington, Washington, was hit by a terrible blizzard. Wellington was a Great Northern Railway stop high in the Cascade Mountains. As much as a foot of snow fell every hour, and on the worst day eleven feet (340 cm) of snow fell.

Two trains, a passenger train and a mail train, both traveling from Spokane to Seattle, were trapped in the local depot. Snowplows were actively at work in Wellington, and others were sent to help, but they could not penetrate the deep accumulations. Matters became worse as more avalanches dumped massive amounts of snow between the towns of Scenic and Leavenworth.

Late on February 28, the snow stopped and was replaced by rain and a warm wind. Just after 1:00 a.m. on March 1, during a violent snowstorm, a slab of snow broke loose from the side of Windy Mountain. A ten-foot-high mass of snow, half a mile long and a quarter of a mile wide, fell toward the town. (Read that again, and try to picture that much snow coming at you.)

The avalanche missed the town's general store and post office, but it hit the railroad depot. Most of the passengers and crew were asleep aboard their trains. The impact threw the trains 150 feet downhill and into the river valley below. Ninety-six people were killed, including thirty-five passengers, fifty-eight Great Northern employees on the trains, and three railroad employees in the depot.

Only twenty-three passengers survived. The work of retrieving bodies was so difficult that it had to be halted for months. Twenty-one weeks later, in late July, it was possible for the last of the bodies to be retrieved.[4]

"PEOPLE DON'T HAVE TO DIE!"

My friend, once again I am weeping. The Wellington avalanche took place over a hundred years ago. Why on earth is it affecting me today? It's because I can't separate the natural from the spiritual. People died in those disasters, and people are dying in today's spiritual disasters.

One of the statements the Colorado ranger made to me was loud and clear: "People don't have to die!" Of course he was speaking of today's avalanches with all our modern-day equipment and warning devices.

I echo that statement: "People don't have to die!"

But they still do.

Having preached the gospel for many decades, I see a common denominator that has risen to the top. Nothing or no one can convince me otherwise. The Lord has given me the privilege of preaching all over the world. We've held meetings with the poorest of the poor and then flown to areas that were dripping with wealth. In many countries I have been treated like a king passing through for a visit. I tell the hosts of those crusades that all I need is a glass of water. Instead, upon arrival I've had five-course meals spread out before me.

I travel to preach the precious Word of God. I often come in fasting and praying. Their hospitality is understood and appreciated, but please, just give me a platform, a place where I can thunder out the truth, a place where Christ will melt their avalanches of idols while melting their hearts of stone.

Regardless of the venue, regardless of the economic position of the country, one thing never changes: the message. "And I, brethren, when I came to you, did not come with excellence of speech or of wisdom declaring to you the testimony of God. For I determined not to know anything among you except Jesus Christ and Him crucified" (1 Cor. 2:1–2). He is the sharpest arrow in my quiver, the most powerful explosive in my arsenal, the One who can annihilate any avalanche, near or far.

The avalanche, left unchecked, will produce hell on the highway. Look past your personal comfort zone, and think about those who have been earmarked by the devil for death. As Christians our calling is much larger than the world around us. Jesus made that clear when He said, "You shall receive power when the Holy Spirit has come upon you; and you shall be witnesses to Me in Jerusalem, and in all Judea and Samaria, and to the end of the earth" (Acts 1:8). Does He need to be more specific? Jesus was pretty specific when He said, "Go into all the world and preach the gospel to every creature" (Mark 16:15).

Why not call yourself a member of the Christian Spiritual Patrol? Whatever your position, stay focused. An alert soldier is constantly scanning his surroundings for the enemy.

> **As Christians our calling is much larger than the world around us.**

These massive murdering mountains of snow are hovering over the spiritual roads that lead to and from Christian sanctuaries. In the natural some of these can be wide interstate highways, freshly scraped and salted, with a steady stream of flowing traffic. And then we have the narrow, two-lane roads that weave throughout the mountains leading to quaint little villages, vacation homes, tiny mom-and-pop ski lodges, and the ever-popular bed-and-breakfast getaways. All of these businesses and dwellings are in danger of destruction.

Spiritually these represent the believers who don't live around the swirl of modern-day Christianity. They might watch Christian television, subscribe to Christian periodicals, or google any rumors, but their nourishment is unlike that of our mainstream buffets. Their spiritual food comes from a country church with a part-time pastor. Oftentimes they depend on an itinerant minister who comes in, preaches, eats a good home-cooked meal, and then moves on. As a watchman keep your eye on everything: "'But if the watchman sees the sword coming and does not blow the trumpet, and the people are not warned, and the sword comes and takes any person from among them, he is taken away in his iniquity; but his blood I will require at the watchman's hand.' So you, son of man: I have made you a watchman for the house of Israel; therefore you shall hear a word from My mouth and warn them for Me" (Ezek. 33:6–7).

If you don't believe these false avalanche words are spreading throughout the world, then keep reading. Areas worldwide are in grave danger of being destroyed by avalanches miles away from the popular Christian tourist attractions. You don't have to be part of a megachurch to be killed by a mountain of falling snow. The false teaching of today has woven its way into the highways and byways of this world.

I'll never forget a pastor calling me from an Eastern Bloc country. I couldn't pronounce the name of his city, but I felt his pain. He was shouting over the phone, "Brother Steve, we live hundreds of miles from any other large city. I have a good church of fifteen hundred faithful members. They fight to live out their faith. Persecution is an everyday threat. Please, Brother Steve, tell the American preachers that they are destroying us. Their teaching doesn't fit here. If they came and lived here, they would see. Do whatever you can to stop the constant false teaching that is pouring in. It is confusing and destroying our people."

I knew exactly what teaching and what teachers he was talking about. He was faithfully preaching biblical holiness and the price of the cross. But the teachings coming over from the Western world were basically teaching the opposite.

My friends, there is only one road that leads to heaven. It is a highway of holiness: "A highway shall be there, and a road, and it shall be called the Highway of Holiness. The unclean shall not pass over it, but it shall be for others. Whoever walks the road, although a fool, shall not go astray" (Isa. 35:8). And with the psalmist we can say, "Open to me the gates of righteousness; I will go through them, and I will praise the LORD. This is the gate of the LORD, through which the righteous shall enter" (Ps. 118:19–20).

Keep an eye on the sides of the road. The heresies are coming down!

This chapter has been an exploration of the similarities between the natural avalanche that slides down and covers the highways, killing all those in its path, and the spiritual avalanche threatening those who are not yet believers or who are coming to Christ around the world. Modern-day false teachers have no clue how many millions could be killed. The Lord has revealed to me that the numbers are in the millions. Their cries have penetrated my heart. The way to Jesus needs to be clean of diabolical debris. Together we will stop the avalanche hovering over the church and do everything we can to halt this hell from falling on the highway to heaven.

We're living in perilous times indeed, and in the next chapter I'll explain how to discern the danger of the hour in which we live.

....

NOTES

1. "Pakistan to Dig Tunnel for Soldiers Buried in Avalanche," *The Telegraph*, April 12, 2012, http://www.telegraph.co.uk/news/ worldnews/asia/pakistan/9199735/Pakistan-to-dig-tunnel-for-soldiers -buried-in-avalanche.html (accessed January 29, 2013).

2. Bridget Johnson, "World's Worst Avalanches: 1950–1951: Winter of Terror," About.com, http://worldnews.about.com/od/ disasters/tp/Worlds-Worst-Avalanches.htm (accessed January 29, 2013).

3. History.com, "December 13, 1916: Soldiers Perish in Avalanche as World War I Rages," http://www.history.com/this-day-in-history/ soldiers-perish-in-avalanche-as-world-war-i-rages (accessed January 29, 2013).

4. Edited from Wikipedia.com, s.v. "Wellington, Washington, Avalanche," http://en.wikipedia.org/wiki/Wellington,_Washington_ avalanche (accessed January 29, 2013).

Chapter 10

SIGNS of the TIMES

YOU'RE NOT GOING TO BELIEVE WHAT THEY'RE TEACHING IN this part of the world!" On the phone was a good friend, known throughout Christendom for his solid biblical teaching. He had just read the avalanche vision and wanted to confirm what I had seen. Although any outside comments are greatly appreciated, they are not necessary for me to continue this work. What has been revealed to me about the times we are living in is without dispute. There is no jury out deliberating on whether or not this is valid truth.

The caller continued, "There are charlatans parading around as qualified teachers, claiming that some of the world's most horrific serial killers are now saved and in heaven." Raising his voice to an almost feverish pitch, he said, "I've never heard such heresy! This is universalism and an abomination to God. Steve, keep standing strong for truth. How can I help you get this word out?" We talked for a few minutes more on what could be done, had a powerful prayer, and said our good-byes. We're both on the same page. Something must be done, and it must be done now!

Most would agree that we are living in dangerous times. The vast majority of people are weighed down with financial fear and are consuming a steady diet of satanic spiritual soup.

I have dedicated a portion of my time to avalanche research, a subject familiar with many readers but foreign in its spiritual application. Actually it's so fascinating that I stand guilty of overloading my brain. But I want you to travel this highway with me.

At times the adventure has been wild and dangerous. The sport of snow skiing brings laughter and tears. Extreme doesn't begin to describe what some daredevils do on the far side of a mountain. The adrenaline rush, lasting but a short while, far exceeds the danger. No one ever thinks they're going to die. "Not me," they'll boast. "I've tackled the highest mountains, the most treacherous terrain, flown headlong into trees, and literally lived only by wearing a helmet."

But there comes a time when even the best are confronted by the worst. If picked up by a slab of rushing snow, the only salvation is to get off that killer wave. Confidence is mixed with overwhelming fear. Skill gives way to hope. When you're suddenly covered, ten feet under, then hope often gives way to panic. Unless a miracle takes place, vehement death is just a few breaths away.

While writing this book I chose to surround myself with visuals that would keep me not only focused but also very factual. One of the items on my desk is a large montage of avalanche signs. These are actual warnings, not something fabricated by my graphics department. While printing up a large picture for me, the woman behind the counter pointed at one with a startled demeanor. She asked, "What is this picture? Are those people dead? Are those body bags?" Sadly the answer was yes. The picture was of a half dozen skiers, dead and zipped up in body bags to be carried down the mountain.

The shock of the clerk in that copy shop sent a chill through my bones. Jeri and I had already witnessed to her, and she had gotten saved. (Read more about how we witness in chapter 12, "They Wouldn't Listen.") Now here she was, oblivious to the book but overtaken by the content.

Now this professionally printed illustration sits in front of me as I write.

PERILOUS TIMES ARE COMING

Question: What flies without wings, hits without hands, and sees without eyes? Answer: An avalanche. This old riddle has been told since the Middle Ages. The people also called it the White Death. They believed these behemoth killers were sent by demons and witches that rode on top of a white blanket of snow. In those days, because there were no warnings, hundreds would die suddenly. In those days, because they had no teachers, everything in its path was destroyed.

Now the warning signs go up early, before we go out. At the resort the trails and slopes are well marked after a storm. The ski patrol has been strategically placing "do or die" signs all over the mountains, such as WARNING: YOU ARE ENTERING AVALANCHE TERRAIN!; CLOSED: AVALANCHE DANGER!; and SKI AREA: BOUNDARY!

> **Question: What flies without wings, hits without hands, and sees without eyes? Answer: An avalanche.**

Just as a concerned pastor, or shepherd, is responsible for wandering sheep, so a well-trained patrol officer is committed to warning all wandering skiers. Ski patrol officers dedicate themselves to safety. Just as skiers must be warned, Christians must be warned.

The Bible clearly cautions us of falling spiritual snow. Prophets of old bellowed out warnings of impending judgments. The trails we walk today are clearly marked. The signposts are strategically placed along our pilgrimage. There are judgments to come, a beautiful heaven and a real hell. Danger awaits if we walk in disobedience.

Here's a well-lit billboard: "Beware of false prophets, who come to you in sheep's clothing, but inwardly they are ravenous wolves" (Matt. 7:15). It's very clear. God has placed hundreds of signs like this in His Word for our spiritual safety, but, sadly, few are heeded.

> **There are judgments to come, a beautiful heaven and a real hell. Danger awaits if we walk in disobedience.**

From the pulpit to the pew there must be a continual cautionary call. We must point to the signs. We must sermonize the signs. We must shout warnings without wavering. Look at the spiritual condition of America and the world when we disregard the signs of the times.

BEWARE OF WOLVES

Just as I have done an intense study on the little foxes that spoil the vine (Song of Sol. 2:15), I have dug into Jesus' warnings of wolves sneaking around the flock. When I decided to study the little foxes, I actually spent two days with a man whose title was "Huntsman." He led a prestigious group of sportsmen who favor fox hunting.

What an incredible two days of uninterrupted teaching, directly from the man who knows everything there is to know about fox hunting! Fox hunting has interested me for years. It's the little things that make us strong and the little things that tear us down.

When Solomon spoke of the little foxes, he was speaking of those little creatures that patiently wait for the keeper of the vineyard to go to sleep or turn his back. These crafty little creatures would sneak in, nibble away at the grapes, devour the leaves, chew on the branches, and even gnaw on the roots until the vine was destroyed.

In Matthew chapter 7 Jesus was speaking of a bigger, more ravenous animal. This one wants blood. This one wants meat. This one wants to kill. So once again I've done a study. It comes out of my concern for the flock. It is one of the most pronounced signs of the times. We have all seen how false teachers have slipped in and killed innocent sheep.

Jesus warned us to beware of ravenous wolves that would lead people astray. Let me repeat the scripture from Matthew 7 I quoted just a few paragraphs ago and include the rest of what Jesus had to say about it.

> Beware of false prophets, who come to you in sheep's clothing, but inwardly they are ravenous wolves. You will know them by their fruits. Do men gather grapes from thornbushes or figs from thistles? Even so, every good tree bears good fruit, but a bad tree bears bad fruit. A good tree cannot bear bad fruit, nor can a bad tree bear good fruit. Every tree that does not bear good fruit is cut down and thrown into the fire. Therefore by their fruits you will know them. Not everyone who says to Me, "Lord, Lord," shall enter the kingdom of heaven, but he who does the will of My Father in heaven. Many will say to Me in that day, "Lord, Lord, have we not prophesied in Your name,

cast out demons in Your name, and done many wonders in
Your name?" And then I will declare to them, "I never knew
you; depart from Me, you who practice lawlessness!"

—MATTHEW 7:15–23

A ravenous wolf is a wild animal that will do anything for something to eat. When I think of ravenous, I think of blood. These animals are extremely hungry and ready to devour whatever moves.
Let me put this in a spiritual context for you. Those ravenous wolves
Jesus spoke of are prophets, pastors, and teachers who will stoop to
any level to fleece the flock.

That's why Jesus said, "Beware!", or watch out. He also said, "They
come to you." He didn't say that they are sent by God.

The sad thing is, in spite of this drastic language, people still per-
sist in deviating from the truth, wandering down dangerous paths
of false prophecy and strange teaching. It reminds me of Paul's
rebuke to the Galatians: "O foolish Galatians, who hath bewitched
you, that ye should not obey the truth, before whose eyes Jesus
Christ hath been evidently set forth, crucified among you?" (Gal.
3:1, KJV). "You ran well. Who hindered you from obeying the truth?"
(Gal. 5:7).

Those wolflike prophets, pastors, and teachers Jesus talked about
are bloodthirsty and live with only one concern: their own well-
being. A little of your money, a little of your attention, a little of
your loyalty…beware! Here are a few more similarities.

- Just as wolves are driven by hunger (thus the phrase
  "hungry as a wolf"), so false prophets are hungry to
  prey upon unsuspecting followers of Jesus.

- Just as wolves are known to travel in packs, so false prophets and teachers are known to surround themselves with those of their own kind.

- Just as wolves are instinctively assertive, always ready to hunt, so false prophets are always ready to point their finger and pounce.

- Just as the wolf's basic nature is selfish and aggressive—which can be seen following a kill or wherever there's a prize involved—so the false prophet and teacher lives under the domineering characteristics of aggression and selfishness.

- Just as a wolf will often move thirty miles between kills, so false prophets stay on the move between kills. When you stay still, you get killed.

- Just as wolves are ravenous animals, tearing apart their victims, so false prophets slip in and leave the church stripped of funds, chaotic in emotion rather than serene, and drained of staying power.

- Just as some wolves are afraid of humans who might fight, so false prophets are afraid of the true man of God, wielding the sword of the Spirit, the Word of God.

- Just as a wolf is willing to take its time, stalking its kill, so false brethren are willing to take their time to capture and kill a member of God's family. (Wolves are known for attacking herds of animals with the intention of separating the larger, more powerful animals from the weaker. We've seen this happen in a spiritual sense during revival.)

I often wonder what some of these teachers would do if there was no blood to be had. If there was no more money in the message—if you took away the cash—would their concern for God's flock all but vanish too?

The vision warned us of advancing snowfall that would potentially create killer avalanches. Just as the serious ski patrols spend countless hours placing warning signs in the proper places, so the Holy Spirit has spoken to countless writers with warnings of the times to come. Hundreds of books and countless sermons have been preached concerning the biblical signs of the times. For us to ignore these dire directions would be foolish. Who do we think we are? Our heavenly Father already is finished with the future. The final act has been written and in heaven has already been played out. Doesn't it make sense to follow the author and finisher to the very end?

When Jesus walked the earth, He knew that His time was limited. If you are a pastor or a church leader, you should feel the same urgency. Slap up the signs, warn the followers, beware of predators, keep alert at all times, and most of all, pay attention to everything that is written in the Word of God! Everything will come to pass!

WE'RE LIVING IN THE END TIMES

The following is not an exhaustive study about the subject. But I do want to share with you some clear scriptural admonitions about the end times. When asked by His disciples, Jesus plainly told them signs that would transpire prior to His return. In these passages Jesus hammered in signposts that would signify the end is near. He hammered with the hope that each warning would sink deep into the soil of every heart.

1. Deception

"Take heed that no one deceives you. For many will come in My name, saying, 'I am the Christ,' and will deceive many" (Matt. 24:4–5).

2. Wars and rumors of wars

"You will hear of wars and rumors of wars. See that you are not troubled; for all these things must come to pass, but the end is not yet. For nation will rise against nation, and kingdom against kingdom.... For false christs and false prophets will rise and show great signs and wonders to deceive, if possible, even the elect" (Matt. 24:6–7, 24).

3. Increased natural disasters

"There will be famines, pestilences, and earthquakes in various places. All these are the beginning of sorrows" (Matt. 24:7–8).

4. A great falling away from the faith

"Let no one deceive you by any means; for that Day will not come unless the falling away comes first" (2 Thess. 2:3).

"Now the Spirit expressly says that in latter times some will depart from the faith, giving heed to deceiving spirits and doctrines of demons, speaking lies in hypocrisy, having their own conscience seared with a hot iron" (1 Tim. 4:1–2).

5. A great increase of wickedness

"But know this, that in the last days perilous times will come: For men will be lovers of themselves, lovers of money, boasters, proud, blasphemers, disobedient to parents, unthankful, unholy, unloving,

unforgiving, slanderers, without self-control, brutal, despisers of good, traitors, headstrong, haughty, lovers of pleasure rather than lovers of God, having a form of godliness but denying its power. And from such people turn away. . . . But evil men and impostors will grow worse and worse, deceiving and being deceived" (2 Tim. 3:1–5, 13).

6. Increased persecution of true Christians

"Then they will deliver you up to tribulation and kill you, and you will be hated by all nations for My name's sake. And then many will be offended, will betray one another, and will hate one another" (Matt. 24:9–10).

"You will be betrayed even by parents and brothers, relatives and friends; and they will put some of you to death" (Luke 21:16).

7. Great increase in knowledge

"But you, Daniel, shut up the words, and seal the book until the time of the end; many shall run to and fro, and knowledge shall increase" (Dan. 12:4).

8. Reestablishment of Israel as a nation

"'I will bring back the captives of My people Israel. . . . I will plant them in their land, and no longer shall they be pulled up from the land I have given them,' says the Lord your God" (Amos 9:14–15).

The sun will always rise in the east, the moon and stars will always fill the evening sky, the waves of the ocean will always roar, and the land and the people of Israel will always be dear to God's heart. They're the ones through whom the end-time revival comes, and they're the ones whom heaven is waiting on to welcome Jesus back to Jerusalem, ushering in His return.

Thus says the LORD,
Who gives the sun for a light by day,
The ordinances of the moon and the stars for a light by night,
Who disturbs the sea,
And its waves roar
(The LORD of hosts is His name):
"If those ordinances depart
From before Me, says the LORD,
Then the seed of Israel shall also cease
From being a nation before Me forever."
—JEREMIAH 31:35–36

For I speak to you Gentiles; inasmuch as I am an apostle to the Gentiles, I magnify my ministry, if by any means I may provoke to jealousy those who are my flesh and save some of them. For if their being cast away is the reconciling of the world, what will their acceptance be but life from the dead?
—ROMANS 11:13–15

O Jerusalem, Jerusalem, the one who kills the prophets and stones those who are sent to her! How often I wanted to gather your children together, as a hen gathers her chicks under her wings, but you were not willing! See! Your house is left to you desolate; for I say to you, you shall see Me no more till you say, "Blessed is He who comes in the name of the LORD!"
—MATTHEW 23:37–39

As the church we have a debt to Israel—they're the people through whom salvation came.

I could wish that I myself were accursed from Christ for my brethren, my countrymen according to the flesh, who are

Israelites, to whom pertain the adoption, the glory, the covenants, the giving of the law, the service of God, and the promises; of whom are the fathers and from whom, according to the flesh, Christ came, who is over all, the eternally blessed God. Amen.

—ROMANS 9:3–5

They are the ones whom we are called to provoke to jealousy.

I say then, have they stumbled that they should fall? Certainly not! But through their fall, to provoke them to jealousy, salvation has come to the Gentiles. Now if their fall is riches for the world, and their failure riches for the Gentiles, how much more their fullness! For I speak to you Gentiles; inasmuch as I am an apostle to the Gentiles, I magnify my ministry, if by any means I may provoke to jealousy those who are my flesh and save some of them.

—ROMANS 11:11–14

Some things never change. Even though God's mercies are new every morning, He never changes, and He keeps His covenant for a thousand generations! The everlasting covenant made with Israel is as valid today as it's ever been. A church that refuses to embrace that covenant is a church that ceases to be all that the Lord's destined it to be.

My friend, there is no need to go any further listing the biblical signs of the times. Hundreds of other books by brilliant authors are available to deepen your understanding of the days we live in. I trust my warnings in this chapter have amply supplied you with what lurks around every God-fearing Christian.

As a strong, evangelistic preacher, I want you to understand how tired I am of rescuing those who should never have wandered off in the first place. They knew better. Not only were they aware of the devil's tactics, but they were also educated on the subject of our own personal weaknesses.

Some things never change. Even though God's mercies are new every morning, He never changes, and He keeps His covenant for a thousand generations!

As I shared earlier, several items surround me as I write this book. One item is a large collage of signs warning of potential avalanches, including a picture of several body bags containing the remains of dead skiers. I look at it constantly. I also have within reach an avalanche probe from Germany. This collapsible rod extends to eleven feet and is used to pierce the snow with the hopes of finding a skier still breathing.

Should the patrol hit a buried skier with this probe, a second item is pulled out of his survival pack. It's a dark red shovel, light in weight but incredible in strength. Mine is called "The Beast." It's also from Germany, an area of the world where avalanches are common. This shovel is designed for one mission: to uncover bodies located by the probe.

Most skiers who have been swept away by these killer waves of snow only have a few minutes to live. Hopefully they were skiing with friends and one of them was fortunate to ride the avalanche down and safely slide off. Now, finding their friend is a daunting task. Knowing that suffocation is imminent makes the rescue a passionate race of life and death.

I can easily compare this rescue to what I do and have done all over the world. I've grabbed the avalanche probe and pierced the snow, hoping to find a breathing backslider or prodigal. Perhaps a sinner who had never known the Lord will be dug up with my small red beast.

Weeping and digging. Digging and weeping. It's what I do and what I'll do as long as breath remains.

Pay close attention to the signs of the times. They have been posted for a purpose.

"Stop! Danger of avalanche: Do not pass this sign!" Don't be "snowed" by a message that tickles the ears and appeals to the eyes but is deadly to the soul.

In the next chapter I'll explain some more deadly aspects of snow and how it relates to the vision and today's church.

Chapter 11

LET IT SNOW!

THERE IS SOMETHING MAGICAL ABOUT THE FIRST SNOWFALL OF the season. Kids clamor with excitement at the prospect of skipping school as the first flakes start to fall. Even adults find it difficult to hold back their inner child when the chance of snow is in the air. Everyone loves snow!

I love waking up in the morning, fresh cup of coffee in hand, staring out the window at the winter wonderland. Just a little snow, and my neighborhood transforms overnight. Lifeless limbs from leafless trees now stand proudly adorned in a fresh dusting of flakes. Rooftops of homes and cars are now decorated with a coat of snow. Even the lawns that had long since turned brown during autumn now glisten in white.

It's not long before little boot prints begin to appear in the fresh blanket of snow as children scurry out to play. Friendly snowmen start to arrive in front of homes, and snowball fights start breaking out across the street. The deadness of winter seems to have come to life all because of a little fresh snow.

Snow is attractive to the eye, but that beauty is deceptive. Most of us have learned that a wintry mix creates a widespread mess!

I live in a city where just an inch of snow can bring the entire region to a halt. One recent morning, as kids played in the snow and I finished my coffee, I retired to the living room to watch the morning news. The scene on TV was so different from the one just outside my window. Hundreds of accidents were scattered throughout the city. A few had been serious. Traffic came to a halt as bridges were impossible to cross. Thousands of homes lost power and no longer enjoyed essential heat. The power company feared that it would be days before all the downed lines were repaired. Local grocery stores were emptied of supplies, and the roads made the prospects of replenishing them unlikely. Businesses were closed, guaranteeing a loss of profit for days. Isn't it strange how something so beautiful to the eye can quickly become so damaging?

The same thing is happening in churches all across the world today. People, like children, have looked to the sky singing "Let It Snow." Pastors have accommodated their request by making sure that the sanctuary glistens with the sights and sounds of a winter wonderland. As the preacher preaches, the saints sit, allowing the soft flakes of his words to fall on them like a blanket of fresh snow. But there is an inherent danger created as the snow continues to fall within the sanctuary.

As unlikely as it may seem, early Arctic explorers experienced continual thirst as they explored regions covered in ice and snow. Some died of dehydration, even though life-giving water was all around. Unfortunately that water was not accessible because it was frozen hard. Even eating the snow was dangerous, as it would lower their body temperature, causing hypothermia.

There is a correlation in the spiritual world. Unwise leaders are creating an environment that is pleasant to the eyes but fails to provide the living water people truly need.

There is a term that was coined many years ago that takes its meaning from this very phenomenon. It's called a "snow job." Very simply, a snow job means "to deceive with insincere talk; false flattery designed to hide truth." A snow job tickles the ears, just as fresh snow appeals to the eye.

That is precisely what the prophet Isaiah spoke about over twenty-five hundred years ago when he said that people would no longer desire the truth of the Lord, desiring to hear only pleasant words and illusions. They "say to the seers, 'Do not see,' and to the prophets, 'Do not prophesy to us right things; speak to us smooth things, prophesy deceits'" (Isa. 30:10).

Years later the apostle Paul wrote to his young protégé Timothy, warning him against such trends in his time.

> I charge you therefore before God and the Lord Jesus Christ, who will judge the living and the dead at His appearing and His kingdom: Preach the word! Be ready in season and out of season. Convince, rebuke, exhort, with all long-suffering and teaching. For the time will come when they will not endure sound doctrine, but according to their own desires, because they have itching ears, they will heap up for themselves teachers; and they will turn their ears away from the truth, and be turned aside to fables. But you be watchful in all things, endure afflictions, do the work of an evangelist, fulfill your ministry.
>
> —2 Timothy 4:1–5

You may have noticed that I've repeated some Scripture texts throughout this book. As an evangelist, and on occasion a teacher, I have learned that most students need to hear a particular lesson many times in different ways. A good, successful teacher will tell the students what he's going to tell them, tell them, and then tell them what he told them.

Paul issued the same type of warning to a group of believers in

Corinth. False doctrine was slipping into that first-century church, threatening to weaken its spiritual foundation. Can you hear the cry of the apostle as he cautioned new believers against that subtle satanic spirit:

> For I am jealous for you with godly jealousy. For I have betrothed you to one husband, that I may present you as a chaste virgin to Christ. But I fear, lest somehow, as the serpent deceived Eve by his craftiness, so your minds may be corrupted from the simplicity that is in Christ. For if he who comes preaches another Jesus whom we have not preached, or if you receive a different spirit which you have not received, or a different gospel which you have not accepted—you may well put up with it!
>
> —2 CORINTHIANS 11:2–4

Why so deadly? Paul referred to Eve's deception in the Garden. She "saw that the tree was good for food, that it was pleasant to the eyes" (Gen. 3:6). Though she had been warned that eating it would bring death, Eve fell for Satan's snow job! The same deception is rampant today in America and all over the world. Pastors and leaders are standing before their congregations snowing the saints with a message that tickles the ears and appeals to the eyes but is deadly to the soul.

LOTS OF AIR WITH LITTLE SUBSTANCE

Did you know that snow is made up mostly of air and very little water? Fresh-fallen snow is 90 to 95 percent air! Not long ago our city received more than a foot of snow. It was welcomed, as our area is prone to extended periods of drought. But when the snow melted, it did nothing for our lack of rain. That foot of snow was worth less than an inch of rain. When it comes to snow, what appears to have so much depth contains very little substance.

Listen to the messages preached from pulpits today. They contain much air and little substance. Feeling the societal pressure to be politically correct, ministers are afraid to deliver the full truth of God's Word for fear of offending. They choose instead to craft messages that impress. But when their words are subjected to the fire of the Word, you find only a few drops of truth.

A few winters ago the kids in my neighborhood made the largest snowman I had ever seen. It had to have taken them hours to create and maneuver those giant snowballs into place, and I have no idea how they managed to lift them on top of one another. According to the record books, the largest snowman ever created was 122 feet tall. It took weeks to construct, and commercial equipment had to be used to complete it.[1] But when the sun came back out, the temperature warmed those impressive creations, they melted away, and nothing remained. So much work for something that didn't last.

God's Word does not melt like snow. It has endured the test of time, has never changed, and remains the same yesterday, today, and forever! The message found in the Word is still the same. Sin is the problem. The blood of Christ is the solution. Repentance is God's method for putting the two together. By the way, if you're a Methodist, Baptist, Episcopalian, Lutheran, Presbyterian, Pentecostal, Catholic, or from any other denominational stream, you believe the gospel story—the penetrating truth of what Jesus Christ had to endure so that we could be redeemed from spiritual death into eternal life through adoption into His family.

Now, two thousand years after His brutal sacrifice, we find pastors snowing the saints with whitewashed messages that will not last to avoid offending society's delicate palates with the bitter truth. It should not be surprising that the critics of Christianity continue to malign the message. It should grieve Christians to the core that His church—which represents His hands, His feet, and His mouth—no longer proclaims the truth.

As a result, those people who desperately need to hear about the love of God must first wade through the drifts of snow before hearing just a drop of truth. I am reminded of the prophet Amos when he bellowed out, "They shall run to and fro, seeking the word of the LORD, but shall not find it" (Amos 8:12).

Jesus wasn't concerned about popularity polls. The only poles that ever affected Him were in the shape of a cross—and even those didn't stop Him from accomplishing His task.

Jesus was never motivated by how His message would be received or by being politically correct to tickle itching ears. He knew there was no value in that. He reduced His congregation to just a faithful few after preaching a heavy message on sacrifice. His words "Eat My flesh and drink My blood" transformed His crowd of cheerleaders into a crowd of cowards. When many walked away, He didn't chase after them. He didn't change His message to cheer them up. When they came singing "Let It Snow," He didn't shower them in a foot of snow. They needed truth.

THE GREATEST SNOW ON EARTH

The state of Utah proudly boasts the motto "Greatest Snow on Earth" on their license plates. Avid skiers and mountain enthusiasts hike into the mountains there to enjoy the snow. A good friend of mine just told me about a couple who were excellent mountaineers. Together they had years of experience in the backcountry hiking to the tops of steep peaks and then descending on fresh, undisturbed snow. But their experience didn't stop them from being engulfed in a 700-foot-wide avalanche. They knew better but said their "judgment was overwhelmed by the pursuit of having more fun and skiing the steeper slopes and the great Utah powder."[2]

Thankfully, when the avalanche came to a halt, the man was only partially covered and able to dig himself out. His girlfriend, however, was lost under feet of snow. He quickly located her using the beacons they were both wearing and dug her out just in time. Later she recounted the feeling of a strange serenity just before she passed out in the snow.[3]

Saints have searched out churches with the best snow. Leaders have gone to great lengths to make sure their slopes are well groomed and appeal to their consumers. Their focus on the snow is blinding everyone to the danger lying beneath the beauty. Even now, as the avalanche begins to bury multitudes, they sit comfortably as a sweet, strange serenity overtakes them. They are completely unaware of the spiritual death that is moments away. The deceiver and enemy of our souls has slithered into the pulpits of America as he did in the garden and is tempting those with itching ears with fresh snow.

The devastating results of slipping away from proclaiming fundamental, doctrinal truths are already evident in our society. We must all feel the responsibility. We must carry the burden. We must share the load if we are to successfully carry out our mandate to this generation. It is essential that we teach the whole counsel of God.

"But," you may ask, "what about the good stuff—like the fact that God wants us to prosper and be in health?" Of course these spiritual benefits are truths found in the Word. But they are the rewards of leading an obedient life. No amount of preaching prosperity to an unbelieving, disobedient crowd will make it happen.

First, people must get right with God! With conversion comes change. This life-altering gospel is summed up in the staunch words of Jesus: "If anyone desires to come after Me, let him deny himself, and take up his cross, and follow Me" (Matt. 16:24).

Perhaps one of the many reasons ministers in churches have become popular is simply because they've lost the sting of the story. It's as if everyone is lured to a gigantic, honey-laden beehive, with no fear of being stung. There are no warrior bees protecting the integrity of the hive. It's all good. It's all sweet. Just scoop some in your hand, slop it down, and soothe your soul.

The sound doctrine Paul referred to is different. It is wholesome doctrine that encourages and contributes to the health and longevity of the soul. It's not just a temporary fix.

> **Pastors who were at one time filled with the power of God now serve up silly sermonettes to Christianettes in bassinets.**

Paul also warned that the day would come when some would not endure, or put up with, sound doctrine. Clearly we have arrived. That time is now! Churches today are filled with people who seek instruction that is more in line with their personal lifestyles, wishes, and desires than with the good of their own souls.

America is slipping into this abyss. Pastors who were at one time filled with the power of God—their voices like trumpets sounding the alarm—now sing sweet lullabies. No more powerful, prophetic words. No more riveting truths that nail sin to the wall and bring freedom. No more crying out to know God with humility and brokenness. Instead they serve up silly sermonettes to Christianettes in bassinets.

Snow the saints and keep them coming back. It is a false and fleeting security. They defend their feel-good messages by claiming their members want to be stroked, not stricken. They want to be pacified. They won't put up with the whole counsel of God. The money won't come in if you offend the givers. The coffers won't fill up unless you speak words they want to hear. The tithers will leave if you confront their sin.

What ridiculous rhetoric! Since when are pastors supposed to allow the pocketbooks in the pews to dictate what they preach in the pulpit? Are we to serve God or mammon?

What parent would allow their children to remain outdoors in the snow too long? Yet, rather than calling the saints inside to be warmed by the Word and refreshed by its truth, pulpit politicians are letting the crowd's desires to stay and play in the snow dictate the message.

The divine drivel of our day reminds me of the trouble the prophet Micah spoke of when he said, "If a liar and deceiver comes and says, 'I will prophesy for you plenty of wine and beer,' he would be just the prophet for this people!" (Mic. 2:11, niv).

Jesus was concerned with heart correctness, not pleasing the political. If preachers are to be relevant and effective, the fluff must be thrown out and replaced with the cross, the blood, repentance, and sacrifice. We must proclaim Jesus Christ and Him crucified for the sins of man.

We must preach change: "Therefore, if anyone is in Christ, he is a new creation; old things have passed away; behold, all things have become new" (2 Cor. 5:17).

The great Bible orators of old never preached slushy, self-centered, society-pleasing sermons. Their words challenged people to live a life of no compromise that included acknowledging and repenting of sin and receiving God's forgiveness.

In the next chapter we'll look at what happens when people don't heed the warnings of the ski patrol and will see the correlation in the spiritual avalanche vision. We need to get back to thundering this message. There are thirsty souls both inside and outside the church who need a fresh drink from the fountain of God. Let's stop trying to offer them, like Utah, the "Greatest Snow on Earth" and instead sound the warning cry until they hear and respond.

. . . .

NOTES

1. Associated Press, "Topping 122 Feet, Snowman in Maine Vies for World Record," FoxNews.com, March 1, 2008, http://www.foxnews.com/story/0,2933,334088,00.html (accessed January 30, 2013).

2. FoxNews.com, "Boyfriend Saves Girlfriend's Life After She Is Buried in Utah Avalanche," January 17, 2013, http://www.foxnews.com/us/2013/01/17/boyfriend-saves-girlfriend-life-after-is-buried-in-utah-avalanche/ (accessed January 30, 2013).

3. Ibid.

Chapter 12

THEY WOULDN'T LISTEN

'VE WRITTEN THIS BOOK TO BE FULL OF GODLY DIRECTION because I want everyone to understand that "blessed are those who keep justice, and he who does righteousness at all times!" (Ps. 106:3). And hopefully my words will help keep people away from the avalanche terrains of today's slippery spiritual slopes.

Daily I hear the cries of those who are suffocating beneath the unexpected snowslide. One former, on-fire young person said the other day, "I can't believe how far I've drifted. All the teaching seemed so safe." I told him to shake off everything that has compromised his life and get back in the battle. He listened to me as a father. He knew that the devil had desired to destroy him.

As I've mentioned before, I have an avalanche probe, a pointed rod used by the ski patrol to find buried skiers in the deep snow. It is a sad but necessary tool. The probe, along with a sharp, snow-piercing shovel, helps to uncover endangered lives. When ski patrol officers find them, many are already dead or are gasping for their last breath. As an evangelist and pastor I've spent my life "piercing the snow," looking for backsliders and prodigals. Sadly, over the years I have also located the spiritually dead—the reprobate—those who have not only left God but also curse His presence in their lives.

My apologies if you've grown weary from my referencing the words of the ski patrol so many times in this book. They have played such an incredible role in analyzing every word in this vision. Hearing their passion for saving lives, much like yours and mine for saving souls, is so edifying and encouraging.

I love passion. The worldly connotation often points to something sexual. But the spiritual application indicates a strong, emotional desire for God, His will, and the purpose for the death of His Son—lost souls.

"They die because they don't listen!" was the cry of the ski patrol. "No one needs to die from an avalanche!" Allow me to share a few recent tragedies that might have been prevented if people had only heeded the warnings.

- A twenty-four-year-old snowboarder died after becoming trapped in an avalanche in a steep Utah backcountry. The public was thoroughly warned to avoid that area after harsh snowstorms. The boarder was with two others when the morning avalanche happened. They watched as their friend descended into the canyon and triggered an avalanche that carried him more than twenty-four hundred feet down the mountain. Less than an hour later they were able to locate him with the help of avalanche beacons, but he was already dead. The director of the Utah Avalanche Center said, "We put out the information, and people are free to use it however they want to. Most heed our advice."[1]

- A pro skier was killed in an avalanche in the backcountry of Utah in an area that was not yet open for the winter season. He knew better but chose to ignore the risk. The skier triggered an avalanche that swept him over a rock cliff. Sadly, this was the second avalanche he'd triggered that day. After having escaped the first, he continued to test fate and paid with his life. His friends said that he pushed himself skiing beyond what anyone would consider safe—and he'd always walked away unscathed.[2]

- In Alberta a backcountry enthusiast in his thirties, along with three friends, entered a dangerous area on a snowmobile for some backcountry downhill skiing. The four were making a descent when an avalanche struck. Three escaped the slide; the other did not. They were properly equipped with backcountry and avalanche gear, but that didn't save his life. The conditions turned bad so quickly that rescue was impossible. Even attempts to recover his body failed.[3]

WE MUST ACT BEFORE IT'S TOO LATE

The avalanche warnings were clear. The warnings in this book are clear. Both are born out of compassion. *Compassion* is a penetrating word meaning "to suffer together."

Ski patrols feel the pain of suffering skiers and are well aware of the last moments before death. They spend time with the families of the lost and take loved ones to the spots where the tragedies occurred. Often a cross, a wreath, or some flowers are placed as simple memorials to a son, daughter, husband, wife, or friend. No one can ease the pain. Words fail. "I tried to warn him" is never uttered. It's too late.

Yes, it is too late for those who have perished. But it's not for those who still have the breath of life.

I remember pulling up to a red light once when I was a young preacher, looking off to my right and seeing a friend who had disappeared from the church and gone his own way. The light was red, and I only had a few minutes. The window went down and I screamed out, "Kevin, so good to see you. Where have you been? I've been praying for you. Pull over and let's talk."

The response he gave was expected. "I've had it with the old-fashioned rules of the church. I want to be free. Just leave me alone, Steve. I'll get right with your God one day." Then he pulled up a bottle that was wedged between his legs. It was hard-core whiskey. He took a swig, chuckled, saw the light turn green, and sped off.

We were both going in the same direction on that four-lane road, and I tried to catch up, but Kevin was obviously trying to get away. He sped out of sight.

My heart broke. He and I had been good friends for more than two years. We'd spent quality time together, praying and seeking God's will for our lives. We had both felt the Lord's call to be evangelists. We were both heading for a lifetime of winning souls. At least, that's what I thought.

Two days later I received a call from another friend. He said, "Have you heard what happened to Kevin? He's dead."

I was shocked, having just seen him. "What happened?" I asked.

"The police say he was speeding over a hundred miles per hour, lost control of his car, slammed into a tree—not wearing a seatbelt. His head hit the windshield, and he died instantly. Steve, he was drunk. They found a bottle in the front seat, and the toxicologist report says he was totally intoxicated."

Another call came in that day from Kevin's family. They asked me to officiate the funeral. I shared with Kevin's mother that I would be honored to help carry his casket and say a few words, but I wasn't prepared to give a sermon. I was young in the Lord and not skilled in delivering messages at funerals where the departed were living away from God. Now, many years later, I know how to deliver a message that touches all those who are present.

I remember it as if it was yesterday. Writing it down is healthy. Reliving the past can often guide us in the future. Stories such as Kevin's are so important for today if they can keep others from making the same mistake.

We all need to listen to warnings.

The ranger's straightforward approach to saving lives is parallel to my own appeal to perishing souls. I adamantly say to you that no one needs to perish. God has made it clear that He desires everyone to come to the knowledge of His Son: "The Lord is not slack concerning His promise, as some count slackness, but is longsuffering toward us, not willing that any should perish but that all should come to repentance" (2 Pet. 3:9).

Allow me to add one more word from His precious love letter to everyone: "Say to them, 'As I live,' says the Lord GOD, 'I have no pleasure in the death of the wicked, but that the wicked turn from his way and live. Turn, turn from your evil ways! For why should you die, O house of Israel?'" (Ezek. 33:11). This is a cry from the heart of God to the heart of man—all men! Everyone!

From the beginning the Lord has sent us a list of rules to follow. All He wants is for us to listen. The simplicity of these rules is almost embarrassing. As the Supreme Being He gave them to us, knowing that without them we would be just wayward wanderers, destined for self-destruction.

Just posting the Ten Commandments in our hearts should be enough to stop our sinfulness and to start living sanctified.

1. Thou shall have no other gods before me.

2. Thou shall not worship idols.

3. Thou shall not take the Lord's name in vain.

4. Remember the Sabbath day, and keep it holy.

5. Honor your father and mother.

6. Thou shall not murder.

7. Thou shall not commit adultery.

8. Thou shall not steal.

9. Thou shall not lie.

10. Thou shall not covet.

Find them in Exodus 20:2–17 and Deuteronomy 5:7–21. Read them as if it's for the first time. Let all the words penetrate your spirit. Why? So God will say, "You listened! You read with your eyes and heard from your heart."

Do you want to make God happy? He makes it clear: "How can a young man cleanse his way? By taking heed according to Your word. With my whole heart I have sought You; oh, let me not wander from Your commandments! Your word I have hidden in my heart, that I might not sin against You" (Ps. 119:9–11).

How about some of those things that God hates? Should we avoid them altogether, or just delete the ones that offend us? Should we listen, should we read, should we obey?

Are you going to read these warning signs and then take off down the spiritual mountain anyway? Is someone going to follow up behind you and pick up the pieces of your shattered, shipwrecked life? Are you going to disregard some of these clear eye-catching signs, watch the avalanche build, and do nothing about it?

For the sake of space I'm going to supply you with just the biblical addresses. Look them up for yourself. For a more exhaustive study check out *Meredith's Book of Bible Lists* by J. L. Meredith (Bethany House). But be forewarned. This is not intended to satisfy those with an insatiable sweet tooth.

Here are just a few scripture warnings you must read:

- Homosexual acts (Lev. 18:22)

- Idols and the materials used to make idols (Deut. 7:25). Note: An idol is anything that takes the place of God, such as fame, fortune, and material possessions.

- Worship of the sun, moon, or stars (Deut. 17:3–4)

- Astrology; fortune-telling (Deut. 18:10)

- Witchcraft (Deut. 18:10)

- Communication with the dead (Deut. 18:11)

- Transvestism (Deut. 22:5)

- Prostitution (Deut. 23:18)

- Dishonesty (Deut. 25:13–16)

- Boastful and wrongdoing (Ps. 5:5)

- Wickedness (Ps. 11:5)

- Love of violence (Ps. 11:5)

- Pride (Prov. 6:16–17)

- Lying (Prov. 6:17)

- Shedding innocent blood (Prov. 6:17)

- Wicked, scheming hearts (Prov. 6:18)

- Rushing to evil (Prov. 6:18)

- False witnesses who speaks lies (Prov. 6:19)

- Sowing discord among brethren (Prov. 6:19)

- Lying lips (Prov. 12:22)

- Ways of the wicked (Prov. 15:9)

- Thoughts of the wicked (Prov. 15:26)

- Proud hearts (Prov. 16:5)

- Justifying the wicked (Prov. 17:15)

- Condemning the just (Prov. 17:15)

- Evil plans against neighbors (Zech. 8:17)

- False oaths (Zech. 8:17)

No, I haven't overlooked all the important signs that Jesus Himself warns us of. After all, it is Jesus we are following, and it is Jesus we should be obeying. His words, backed up by His actions, are undeniable. That's why I dedicated all of chapter 13 to Jesus' words, which appear in red in the Scriptures. Three passages that deserve notice here as well include the following.

> He who has My commandments and keeps them, it is he who loves Me. And he who loves Me will be loved by My Father, and I will love him and manifest Myself to him.
>
> —John 14:21

If you keep My commandments, you will abide in My love, just as I have kept My Father's commandments and abide in His love.

—John 15:10

Do not think that I came to destroy the Law or the Prophets. I did not come to destroy but to fulfill. For assuredly, I say to you, till heaven and earth pass away, one jot or one tittle will by no means pass from the law till all is fulfilled. Whoever therefore breaks one of the least of these commandments, and teaches men so, shall be called least in the kingdom of heaven; but whoever does and teaches them, he shall be called great in the kingdom of heaven.

—Matthew 5:17–19

IT'S NOT OKAY—
IT'S TIME TO OBEY!

But sadly, like the warnings of the ski patrol, we read the Scripture warnings—including the words of Jesus—and we even understand their seriousness, but we don't obey.

One day a little boy came running up to me with tears in his eyes. He was crying uncontrollably over a story he had read in my small testimony book, *Stone Cold Heart*. We have distributed hundreds of thousands of these evangelistic booklets all over the world, in many languages. The response has been beyond my wildest dreams. It's simple. Genuine conviction from young and old makes all our efforts worthwhile.

The boy grabbed my arm, pulled me toward him, and with all the passion a little boy could muster, he screamed out, "Are you Mr. Hill?"

I said, "Yes." Trembling at meeting the author, he said, "My name is Robert, and I have sinned! I'm so sorry." He was obviously torn to pieces over his wrongdoing. My mind immediately raced to some hideous crime that even a young boy might commit. He clearly wanted to confess something, and it couldn't wait.

"Robert," I replied, "thank you for reading my booklet. I wrote it for young people just like you. What is it that has caused you to come? You can talk to me. I will listen."

"Mr. Hill," he said, "I read your story about stealing cookies from the cookie jar. When you were a boy, my age, you grabbed some warm cookies while your mother wasn't looking. She told you to stay away from them; they would spoil your appetite. Later on you took them to your room, ate them, and then felt bad over what you did. That's how I feel. I didn't steal cookies. I did something much worse."

Not knowing what he was going to confess, I braced myself for the unthinkable. Could it be a violent crime? A major drug deal with older friends? A robbery involving guns? Then he dropped his head and confessed, "I stole a dollar from my mommy's purse. She doesn't know. I feel so bad after reading your book. You talk about sin, and I know I'm a sinner. I want Jesus to forgive me."

Before continuing, I want to warn everyone about situations of this nature. Just because you might have a hardened, calloused conscience doesn't mean others have lost their innocence. This boy was a real, breathing child of God. He wasn't a thing or a number; he was a little lamb who wanted the shelter of a shepherd.

And his conviction was biblical. He disobeyed his mother (broke the fifth commandment), he stole some money (broke the eighth commandment), and he lied by keeping it a secret (broke the ninth commandment). Who are we to brush this off as some insignificant boyish prank that he would grow out of? No, my friend. If he hardens his heart as a child, he will have a heart of stone as an adult. I *always* take every altar call, conviction, tear, sorrow, and violated conscience seriously.

I knelt down to his height and said, "Jesus will forgive you, Robert, because He loves you. But you must confess to your mom, ask her to forgive you, and then see if you can work around the house to pay her back." We prayed, and I signed his book with some encouraging words.

Robert followed my instructions, did exactly as I said, and came up to me a few days later, totally changed. His countenance was radiating Jesus. This whole incident can be explained by this passage: "A merry heart makes a cheerful countenance, but by sorrow of the heart the spirit is broken" (Prov. 15:13). He came to me a broken little boy and left with the joy of the Lord, full of peace, enjoying forgiveness. That all happened because he read what to do and obeyed. He listened.

Can you imagine what would happen if everyone began obeying the Lord? That is what the vision is all about. I have been instructed of the Lord to hit the problem head-on. The way we fix the problem is how little Robert fixed his problem. We recognize our failure, repent, make restitution, and move on.

Imagine if Robert had gone to his friends instead of coming to me or another godly pastor? They would have probably said something like, "It's okay, Robert. It's just a dollar. No big deal."

Every major sin starts with a minor sin.

Just a layer of snow—no big deal. So Robert covers it up. He doesn't confess, and he repeats the offense. The next time it's two dollars—another layer of snow.

Don't laugh, my friend, and don't dare make fun of the little sins. Every major sin starts with a minor sin. Hard-core criminals start early on, many of them with just a dollar from a purse. I have worked for years with hardened criminals. They were all once just little boys and little girls.

For some the avalanche layers start early. People have friends who take them down an easy path. Or maybe false teachers who steadily lead them astray, saying, "It's okay! Don't worry about it."

Consider the life of King David: First it was just a look, then a call for the woman, then an affair, then the consequences of the affair, then killing her husband to cover it up. Then, thank God, the entrance of Nathan the prophet, who detected layers upon layers of sin. The sin, or snow, would have crashed down on David like an avalanche had it not been for the wise warning of that man of God!

I received a call from a distraught woman of God. She and her husband are dear friends of mine. She had just walked out of a women's meeting where the speaker informed the attendees that this year was going to be a year of great prosperity and personal blessings. Knowing instead that the year was going to be filled with persecution and intense spiritual warfare, she couldn't stomach the teaching any longer and politely walked out. She knew the prophetess very well and was expecting a call soon. The question would arise: Why did she walk out?

When she called me for advice, my response was the same as always: speak the truth in love. I told her to share what God was saying to her and say that she totally disagreed with what the speaker was offering the ladies. No arrogance. Just share her heart. It isn't time for peace, joy, and prosperity. It's time to take up arms and take back our children, our families, our schools, our government, and our nation. Anyone worldwide who doesn't see that has been blinded by the god of this day.

I told her the snow's going to fall, but we must raise up our voices and let the people know that it won't stick. Not on our watch. I will fight to the bitter end. Actually, I'm going to fight to the *better* end. We win, and it's an incredible Jesus-honoring victory.

"They won't listen to me," says the pastor.

"They won't listen to me," says the teacher.

"They won't listen to me," says the evangelist.

"They won't listen to me," says the prophet.

"They won't listen to me," says the apostle.

"They won't listen to me," says the church deacon.

"They won't listen to me," says the parishioner.

Oh, yes, they will! The Bible doesn't say *everyone* won't endure sound doctrine. It says *many*. There are countless people whose hearts are tender. They will listen to your instructions and will yield to your counsel.

How do I know this? Not only from years of experience but also from precious fruit all over this planet. Some of those who threw the tomatoes are now my most-trusted disciples. They're out there. Just make sure you are speaking loud and clear.

I have some good news from the snow-covered, avalanche-prone mountains. The majority of the skiers take heed and listen to the rangers.

They come up to them and say, "Thank you for saving my life." They will come up to you and say, "Thank you for taking the time to instruct me about false teaching. Because you poured out your heart, I have the genuine joy of the Lord. I'm living holy, not because I have to, but because I want to."

They will thank you for pointing directly at that mountain and saying, "Be careful; you're standing below a potential spiritual avalanche that could destroy your life and the lives of millions."

In the next chapter we'll look at the scriptures that we must use as a measure of all of the teaching we hear in the church today: the words of Jesus, or as I call them, "the words in red."

....

NOTES

1. Martin Griffith, "Snowboarder Dies in Avalanche in Utah," *Denver Post*, January 28, 2012, http://www.denverpost.com/legislature/ci_19842933 (accessed January 30, 2013).

2. Jason Blevins, "Jamie Pierre, Utah Pro Skier, Dies in Avalanche in Snowbird Ski Area," *All Things Colorado Sports* (blog), DenverPost.com, November 14, 2011, http://blogs.denverpost.com/sports/2011/11/14/jamie-pierre-dead-utah-avalanche/20458/ (accessed January 30, 2013).

3. *Vancouver Sun*, "Alberta Skier Dies in Avalanche," January 5, 2010, http://www.canada.com/vancouversun/news/westcoastnews/story.html?id=30d4e432-5be3-4c6a-aff4-81292e71a232 (accessed January 30, 2013).

Chapter 13

ALL the WORDS in RED

A YOUNG GERMAN IMMIGRANT NAMED LOUIS KLOPSCH WAS working in New York as an editor for a trade publication in 1899. Klopsch was reading his Bible when Luke 22:20 caught his eye, "This cup is the new testament in my blood, which is shed for you" (KJV).

Klopsch was riveted by the symbolism in Christ's words. A simple yet bold idea fell into his spirit that would forever change the way Bibles are printed. Klopsch envisioned printing the words of Christ in blood-red ink. He asked a trusted spiritual mentor of his if the idea would be permissible. The leader responded, "It could do no harm, and it most certainly could do much good."

Klopsch printed an initial sixty thousand copies of *The Red Lettered Testament* and sold out immediately. The idea was an overnight success and became so well received that nearly every Bible since has been printed with red letters.[1]

This God-given idea certainly could do much good, but only if the reader is careful to read and heed all the words in red! Sadly pastors, preachers, and parishioners are guilty of ignoring many of Christ's red-lettered words. Skillful speakers lift verses out of God's perfect and complete Word that appeal to their tastes or fit the latest revelation they wish to peddle. They skip over or completely ignore other scriptures that don't fit their context or challenge their point. These carefully crafted messages may be appealing to the uninformed saints, but it's appalling to the Savior.

There is a simple remedy for this condition, and it's found written in bold red letters. Pastor, are you preaching all the words in red? Saint, are you taking heed of every red-lettered word Jesus spoke? Is it possible that you have omitted some of Christ's words by concentrating more on His pleasant teachings over the harsher ones? I challenge you to look anew upon His words and let them go through you. The words in red reveal a bolder image of Christ than the one currently preached in so many pulpits.

WE NEED A BOLDER IMAGE OF JESUS

The image of Christ painted by the red-lettered words is so different from the painted image of Jesus that hangs on so many church walls. Artists from the Renaissance imagined this transcendent Jesus with flowing locks of brown hair, blue eyes, and effeminate features. I see a much bolder Jesus when I read the Word.

John the Baptist introduced Jesus as a man "whose sandals I am not worthy to carry. He will baptize you with the Holy Spirit and fire. His winnowing fan is in His hand, and He will thoroughly clean out His threshing floor, and gather His wheat into the barn; but He will burn up the chaff with unquenchable fire" (Matt. 3:11–12; see also Luke 3:16–17).

When John the Beloved described Jesus in the book of Revelation, he said:

> I saw…someone "like a son of man," dressed in a robe reaching down to his feet and with a golden sash around his

chest. His head and hair were white like wool, as white as snow, and his eyes were like blazing fire. His feet were like bronze glowing in a furnace, and his voice was like the sound of rushing waters. In his right hand he held seven stars, and out of his mouth came a sharp double-edged sword. His face was like the sun shining in all its brilliance.

—Revelation 1:12–16, NIV

This is no puny Savior; He is a majestic King and a victorious Warrior. He is an awesome God who is both beautiful and frightening to behold. When this Jesus spoke, John said His voice thundered like the torrent of a mighty waterfall. John caught just a glimpse of Jesus in all His glory and immediately hit the ground as though dead.

Then, recorded in red letters, Jesus commissioned John, "Do not be afraid. I am the First and the Last. I am the Living One; I was dead, and behold I am alive for ever and ever! And I hold the keys of death and Hades. Write, therefore, what you have seen, what is now and what will take place later" (vv. 17–19, NIV).

This disciple whom Jesus loved was trusted with the final written words of Christ in Scripture. He took great care to capture and accurately transcribe every letter of every word. He guarded each of them as precious gems worth greater value than any earthly treasure. He preserved them so that he could present them in all their brilliance to all who would follow.

You and I must do the same. We must once again glimpse the glory of our awesome Savior until we find ourselves struck with awe and fear by His incomprehensible majesty. We must consume every single one of His precious words so that we may guard each of them within our heart and herald them for all who will listen.

There is a powerful revelation of the reality of the Son of God waiting for you to discover if you'll just read the words in red!

THE WORDS IN RED

Read the words printed in red in your Bible, and you will discover a Jesus who is drastically different from the Jesus preached from so many pulpits. Jesus was a radical man who preached a bold message. He confronted the popular teachings of the day, and He challenged the religious rituals that kept the people in bondage. He never held back and He never backed down.

Look at His words here from Matthew and imagine this message being preached next Sunday at your church.

> The teachers of the law and the Pharisees sit in Moses' seat. So you must obey them and do everything they tell you. But do not do what they do, for they do not practice what they preach. They tie up heavy loads and put them on men's shoulders, but they themselves are not willing to lift a finger to move them. Everything they do is done for men to see.
> —MATTHEW 23:2–5, NIV

Jesus then chastised the Pharisees with eight strongly worded statements that begin with "Woe to you" as He called them out by name:

1. Hypocrites (Matt. 23:13–15, 23, 25, 27, 29)

2. A son of hell (v. 15)

3. Blind (vv. 16–17, 19, 24, 26)

4. Fools (vv. 17, 19)

5. Whitewashed tombs (v. 27)

6. Sons of those who murdered the prophets (v. 31)

7. Serpents (v. 33)

8. Brood of vipers (v. 33)

He had no issue with calling people out. He once called King Herod "that fox" and false prophets "ravenous wolves" (Luke 13:32; Matt. 7:15). Today we are so restrained by political correctness that if Jesus stepped up to the pulpit and called out names, most in the audience would cringe.

Jesus wrapped this positive message up by asking the Pharisees, "How can you escape the condemnation of hell?" (Matt. 23:33).

> **Today we are so restrained by political correctness that if Jesus stepped up to the pulpit and called out names, most in the audience would cringe.**

HELL IS REAL AND PEOPLE NEED TO KNOW IT!

Hell is a subject strangely absent from most pulpits today. When is the last time you heard a message on hell? But Jesus spoke of hell, judgment, and punishment often. The popularity-seeking pastor may strain with all his humanistic ingenuity to explain away the reality of these words in red. However, the truth contained within them is plainly seen:

> I say to you that whoever is angry with his brother without a cause shall be in danger of the judgment.
> —MATTHEW 5:22

Whoever says, "You fool!" shall be in danger of hell fire.

—MATTHEW 5:22

It is more profitable for you that one of your members perish, than for your whole body to be cast into hell.

—MATTHEW 5:30;
SEE ALSO MARK 9:43–47

Every tree that does not bear good fruit is cut down and thrown into the fire.

—MATTHEW 7:19

I say to you that many will come from east and west, and sit down with Abraham, Isaac, and Jacob in the kingdom of heaven. But the sons of the kingdom will be cast out into outer darkness. There will be weeping and gnashing of teeth.

—MATTHEW 8:11–12

The Son of Man will send out His angels, and they will gather out of His kingdom all things that offend, and those who practice lawlessness, and will cast them into the furnace of fire.

—MATTHEW 13:41–42

So it will be at the end of the age. The angels will come forth, separate the wicked from among the just, and cast them into the furnace of fire.

—MATTHEW 13:49–50

The master of that servant will come on a day when he is not looking for him and at an hour that he is not aware of, and will cut him in two and appoint him his portion with the hypocrites. There shall be weeping and gnashing of teeth.

—MATTHEW 24:50–51

Cast the unprofitable servant into the outer darkness. There will be weeping and gnashing of teeth.

—MATTHEW 25:30

Then He will also say to those on the left hand, "Depart from Me, you cursed, into the everlasting fire prepared for the devil and his angels."

—MATTHEW 25:41

But He will say, "I tell you I do not know you, where you are from. Depart from Me, all you workers of iniquity." There will be weeping and gnashing of teeth.

—LUKE 13:27–28

If anyone does not abide in Me, he is cast out as a branch and is withered; and they gather them and throw them into the fire, and they are burned.

—JOHN 15:6

Study the words in red, and you will see that Jesus had one message: "Repent, for the kingdom of heaven is at hand" (Matt. 4:17). Every parable, every sermon, every truth was a divine attempt to correct mankind's wayward path and set it back toward the kingdom of God. Jesus, the evangelist, never stopped telling people to turn from their sin and turn toward God. He didn't just speak of the eternal life that awaited those who listened, but He also spoke of the everlasting punishment that awaited those who refused (Matt. 25:46).

Messages on God's blessings, prosperity, and reward abound. They sell books and fill sanctuaries. But what about God's discipline, judgment, penalties, and punishments?

The parable of the talents is most often preached about the reward waiting those who faithfully use their gifts, talents, and resources

God has entrusted to them. Everyone wants to hear Jesus say, "Well done, good and faithful servant! You have been faithful with a few things; I will put you in charge of many things. Come and share your master's happiness!" (Matt. 25:14–30; see also Luke 19:12–27).

What about the penalty awaiting those who squander away their gifts by doing nothing? The foolish servant is rarely focused on for more than a few thoughts. Pastors, take note and be sure that your parishioners know the penalty of not using their talent.

> From him who does not have, even what he has will be taken away. And cast the unprofitable servant into the outer darkness. There will be weeping and gnashing of teeth.
> —MATTHEW 25:29

Every parable, every sermon, every truth was a divine attempt to correct mankind's wayward path and set it back toward the kingdom of God.

Read His red-lettered words! Jesus is greatly concerned that each of us bears fruit and brings a return for the Word He has entrusted to us! Some might say, "Doesn't His grace accept me just as I am?" Yes. But His grace is too powerful to leave you as you are. His grace will work through you to produce fruits of righteousness, but His grace does not mean that He will patiently wait forever for a well-planted, watered, and fertilized tree to bear fruit. Let's look at how Jesus put it.

> A certain man had a fig tree planted in his vineyard, and he came seeking fruit on it and found none. Then he said to the keeper of his vineyard, "Look, for three years I have come

seeking fruit on this fig tree and find none. Cut it down; why
does it use up the ground?" But he answered and said to him,
"Sir, let it alone this year also, until I dig around it and fertilize
it. And if it bears fruit, well. But if not, after that you can cut
it down."

—LUKE 13:6–9

God's matchless grace cannot cover those who, because of their
love for the darkness, run from the light and refuse to receive the
glorious gift of Jesus Christ for their salvation. Saint, run from any
teacher or teaching that creates the notion that a fruitless life will
escape the fire! God's grace is not a big cover-up for an unholy life.
Jesus did not die a gruesome death on a rugged cross, shedding
His precious blood to give you a life free to live however you please.
Your life is not your own. It's been bought by a great price, and only
those lives robed in His righteousness will find eternal reward:

When the king came in to see the guests, he saw a man there
who did not have on a wedding garment. So he said to him,
"Friend, how did you come in here without a wedding garment?" And he was speechless. Then the king said to the ser-
vants, "Bind him hand and foot, take him away, and cast him
into outer darkness; there will be weeping and gnashing of
teeth." For many are called, but few are chosen.

—MATTHEW 22:11–14

This radical message was no more welcomed two thousand years
ago than it is now. When Jesus spoke these words, the Pharisees
were enraged. They rejected His words, while the people rejoiced in
them (Mark 11:18). The religious sought a way to destroy them and
keep them from the people. Don't be guilty of doing the same!

A WORD FOR PASTORS

Let me speak for a moment to pastors reading this book. Pastor, you are an under-shepherd of the Great Shepherd. You've been enlisted as a watchman entrusted to guard His flock and tend to His house. Your job is that of a doorkeeper. Make sure you do your job well! Look at Jesus' words.

> Most assuredly, I say to you, he who does not enter the sheep-fold by the door, but climbs up some other way, the same is a thief and a robber. But he who enters by the door is the shepherd of the sheep. To him the doorkeeper opens, and the sheep hear his voice; and he calls his own sheep by name and leads them out. And when he brings out his own sheep, he goes before them; and the sheep follow him, for they know his voice. Yet they will by no means follow a stranger, but will flee from him, for they do not know the voice of strangers.
>
> —John 10:1–5

I had the opportunity to preach on the steps of the old temple in the heart of Jerusalem. As I stood there and proclaimed the gospel, I was overwhelmed with the thought that Jesus stood in a spot exactly like this when He drove out the moneychangers. That was a violent event as the Great Shepherd ran the thief and robber out of the temple. Jesus' own disciples commented on the zeal Christ displayed for God's house. He didn't whisper. He didn't politely ask those men to leave. He was a man consumed with righteous anger. Armed with a whip, He forcefully removed those who would take advantage of God's people as He said:

It is written, "My house shall be called a house of prayer," but
you have made it a "den of thieves."
—MATTHEW 21:13

Pastor, read the words in red! If Jesus were to attend your church
this weekend, how many tables would be overturned? How many
leaders would He have to whip? Would this radical be welcomed
through your doors or ushered out of them? Has Jesus been given
unrestricted access to your own heart? What would He overturn or
seek to drive out? How will you respond when this radical Jesus is
set loose in your own life? Will you reject His words, or will you
rejoice in them?

Is this image of Jesus in line with the messages you're hearing
preached? Don't misunderstand me. I am not seeking to make Jesus
mean. I am simply seeking to complete the picture.

Everyone loves the picture of Christ with a child on His lap as
He teaches us to become like a child:

Assuredly, I say to you, unless you are converted and become
as little children, you will by no means enter the kingdom of
heaven. Therefore whoever humbles himself as this little child
is the greatest in the kingdom of heaven. Whoever receives
one little child like this in My name receives Me.
—MATTHEW 18:3–5;
SEE ALSO MARK 9:33–37; LUKE 9:46–48

It is a beautiful image of Christ. Do a quick image search online
of "Jesus children." Thousands upon thousands of pictures will be
displayed of our loving Savior embracing children like the perfect
father He is. I have several pictures like these created by master artists from centuries ago. But this can't be the only way we see Christ.

Keep reading the words in red. With a child still on His lap Jesus warns:

> But whoever causes one of these little ones who believe in Me to sin, it would be better for him if a millstone were hung around his neck, and he were drowned in the depth of the sea. Woe to the world because of offenses! For offenses must come, but woe to that man by whom the offense comes!
>
> —MATTHEW 18:6–7

I've seen millstones with my own eyes. They are scattered throughout the Holy Land. Most weigh more than two tons. Pastor, do you understand the implications of ignoring all of Jesus' words in red? Are you causing your people to stumble because you refuse to preach the whole Word? Is there a millstone with your name on it?

Just the other day I was having a polite conversation with a pastor of a large church. I asked him how his church was doing. He responded quickly, "Oh, Steve, everything is great." He said it so proudly that I knew something was off. Everything is "great"? What are you preaching? Are you preaching all the words in red? Surely you're ticking somebody off. Surely not everyone loves you.

In fact, Jesus assured His disciples that they would be hated by the world.

> If the world hates you, you know that it hated Me before it hated you. If you were of the world, the world would love its own. Yet because you are not of the world, but I chose you out of the world, therefore the world hates you. Remember the word that I said to you, "A servant is not greater than his

master." If they persecuted Me, they will also persecute you. If
they kept My word, they will keep yours also.

—JOHN 15:18–20

The lack of persecution could be a telling symptom of our spiritual condition. Do you grasp the implication of Christ's words? If
everybody loves you, what does that say about the kingdom you
belong to? Jesus spoke clearly of the cost of following Him.

If anyone desires to come after Me, let him deny himself, and
take up his cross, and follow Me. For whoever desires to save
his life will lose it, but whoever loses his life for My sake will
find it. For what profit is it to a man if he gains the whole
world, and loses his own soul? Or what will a man give in
exchange for his soul?

—MATTHEW 16:24–26

Leaders today are frantically trying to create a no-cost cross. We
want Christianity without sacrifice, heaven without holiness, and
worldliness without consequence. Jesus didn't leave any middle
ground. His Words were clear.

> **The church is working hard to make friends
> with the world, but to be friends with
> the world is to be enemies with God.**

Pastor, do you have enemies? Are you hated? Does everyone sing
your praises? Do you have people who mock you, ridicule you, say
hateful things about you? If not, are you sure you're preaching all
the words in red?

Not everyone is going to like you; many are going to hate you.

The church is working hard to make friends with the world, but to be friends with the world is to be enemies with God. A good friend of mine just told me of a preacher who was teaching his people to "go have a beer" with someone when they publicly reject you. Friend, that is worldly wisdom. Jesus said something quite opposite.

> Whoever will not receive you nor hear your words, when you depart from that house or city, shake off the dust from your feet. Assuredly, I say to you, it will be more tolerable for the land of Sodom and Gomorrah in the day of judgment than for that city!
>
> —Matthew 10:14–15;
> see also Mark 6:11; Luke 9:5

The words in red paint a picture of a Savior so drastically different from the one preached in pulpits these days. Everyone wants to see Jesus as a gentle Shepherd, lovingly stroking the head of little sheep. We all love His strokes. But we need His *strikes* as well. It would do each of us a world of good to be taken out to God's woodshed from time to time to be disciplined by Jesus.

Jesus always balanced His messages with strokes and strikes. The Sermon on the Mount begins with great blessings:

- Blessed are the poor in spirit.
- Blessed are those who mourn.
- Blessed are the meek.
- Blessed are those who hunger and thirst for righteousness.
- Blessed are the merciful.
- Blessed are the pure in heart.

- Blessed are the peacemakers.

- Blessed are those who are persecuted because of righteousness.

- Blessed are you when people insult you, persecute you, and falsely say all kinds of evil against you (Matt. 5:3–11).

If Jesus had stopped there, everyone would have loved Him. People would have responded to the message, "Isn't it wonderful; we are all so blessed! Moses cursed us with the law, but Jesus has blessed us with grace." We all love His strokes.

Then, like a good father, Jesus pulled out the rod to deliver His strike:

> You have heard that it was said to those of old, "You shall not murder, and whoever murders will be in danger of the judgment." But I say to you that whoever is angry with his brother without a cause shall be in danger of the judgment. And whoever says to his brother, "Raca!" shall be in danger of the council. But whoever says, "You fool!" shall be in danger of hell fire.
>
> —Matthew 5:21–22

He continued:

> You have heard that it was said to those of old, "You shall not commit adultery." But I say to you that whoever looks at a woman to lust for her has already committed adultery with her in his heart.
>
> —Matthew 5:27–28

Oh, how He loves us! If He didn't love us, He wouldn't discipline us. His love compelled Him to confront our sin. He called it out of the deep recesses of the heart. He didn't excuse their sin or dismiss it. He said to deal with it:

> If your right eye causes you to sin, pluck it out and cast it from you; for it is more profitable for you that one of your members perish, than for your whole body to be cast into hell. And if your right hand causes you to sin, cut it off and cast it from you; for it is more profitable for you that one of your members perish, than for your whole body to be cast into hell.
>
> —Matthew 5:29–30

Some have suggested that Jesus was speaking metaphorically, or figuratively, in an attempt to soften the tone of His words. Don't reject His words! Jesus said what He meant and meant what He said. He was speaking clearly of the seriousness of sin and the necessity of dealing with it decisively. If these red words, His words, are causing you some discomfort, don't run from it or dismiss it. Deal with it!

FOR GOD SO LOVED THE WORLD

John 3:16 is the most-quoted scripture on Planet Earth. I've shared Christ with men who just stepped out of a bar, covered in the stench of alcohol in a drunken stupor, and could still quote, "For God so loved the world…" Sinful people love to comfort themselves with the notion that God loves them. But the verse that tells us of God's love is the same verse that shares His judgment as well. Read all the words in red:

For God so loved the world that He gave His only begotten Son, that whoever believes in Him should not perish but have everlasting life. For God did not send His Son into the world to condemn the world, but that the world through Him might be saved. He who believes in Him is not condemned; but he who does not believe is condemned already, because he has not believed in the name of the only begotten Son of God. And this is the condemnation, that the light has come into the world, and men loved darkness rather than light, because their deeds were evil. For everyone practicing evil hates the light and does not come to the light, lest his deeds should be exposed. But he who does the truth comes to the light, that his deeds may be clearly seen, that they have been done in God.

—JOHN 3:16–21

John 3:16 is just as much a judgment scripture as it is a love scripture. These words in red tell us that we were perishing. We were already condemned. The verdict was in; the judgment was made. We loved the darkness and hated the light. Yet in spite of all that stood against us, God so loved us that He sent His Son, the Deliverer.

Many ask, how could a loving God send anyone to hell? Yet the very verse that so many know and misquote answers the question. He didn't come to condemn the world; we were already condemned. He didn't come to send anyone to hell; we were already headed there.

He came to deliver us from hell. Those who listen to His words, Jesus tells us, will not perish but have eternal life. Those who do not listen are already condemned.

I thank God for the hope found in the red letters. His words saved my life. He sacrificed His life and spilled His blood to save me from my sin. Every drop of His blood is priceless. How dare anyone have the audacity to cheapen His sacrifice by ignoring a single one of His red-lettered words!

As I write this, I'm staring at a picture sitting on my desk of six makeshift body bags fashioned from sleeping bags. Each is tagged with the name of a deceased skier. This picture is the last taken of these six men and women. I've referred to this heartbreaking picture a few times in this book because it keeps me focused on what is really happening in the Christian world. Perhaps just the mention of it will do the same for you.

That group of friends chose not to heed the warnings clearly posted on the mountain. Each of them consciously made the decision to climb around a roadblock filled with warning signs that clearly separated the safe path down the mountain from the dangerous backcountry. The signs stated in bold red letters, "Stop! Avalanche Danger! Do Not Cross." Yet those six thrill seekers chose not to heed the warnings and continued walking in a condemned direction. They didn't think it could happen to them. They didn't know that their dreams and futures would end that day. There was an avalanche about to happen, and it took them out. Ignoring the words written in red cost them their lives.

Tears fill my eyes as I write this. My heart breaks for the families and for the lives lost. And I'm reminded of another parable Jesus told.

> The ground of a certain rich man yielded plentifully. And he thought within himself, saying, "What shall I do, since I have no room to store my crops?" So he said, "I will do this: I will pull down my barns and build greater, and there I will store all my crops and my goods. And I will say to my soul, 'Soul, you have many goods laid up for many years; take your ease; eat, drink, and be merry.'" But God said to him, "Fool! This

night your soul will be required of you; then whose will those things be which you have provided?"

—LUKE 12:16–20

Friend, ignoring the words written in red will cost you as well. Pastor, omitting the words written in red will cost you and your people. Preach all the red-letter words. Saint, open the Word and ask the Holy Spirit to breathe fresh life upon Christ's words. These red-lettered words will do you much good! Let them go through you like the sharp sword that they are. Let the radical words of Jesus deliver you from the spiritual avalanche that awaits everyone who foolishly chooses to ignore what is plainly posted in bold red letters!

Next we'll look at some of the foundational teachings of the gospel that have seemingly gone by the wayside. If we are to start believing all the words in red, we must get back to the basics of the gospel and share the truth with everyone who will listen.

NOTES

1. Steve Eng, "The Story Behind: Red Letter Bible Editions," *Bible Collector's World*, January/March 1986, http://www.biblecollectors .org/articles/red_letter_bible.htm (accessed January 30, 2013).

Chapter 14

"I USED to BELIEVE THAT STUFF"

T AKE A TRIP WITH ME DOWN MEMORY LANE. REMEMBERING what God has done in our lives is spiritually healthy for everyone. Even some of the difficult times are good to rehearse so you can see what the Lord has brought you through. The psalmist said, "I will remember the works of the LORD; surely I will remember Your wonders of old. I will also meditate on all Your work, and talk of Your deeds" (Ps. 77:11–12).

Perhaps we should all take the stand of King David when it comes to difficult spiritual understanding: "Such knowledge is too wonderful for me; it is high, I cannot attain it" (Ps. 139:6). He faced the fact that he was a mere mortal and that God is wonderfully immortal. God is the One and Only who knows it all.

I'll never forget how I came to the Lord, back in 1975. The details are as vivid and clear to me today as if it had just happened yes-terday. I was radically saved while on my deathbed due to major drug abuse. My body had been in violent convulsions for three straight days and nights. I knew I was dying. In desperation my mother called a Lutheran vicar for help. He came into my room and spoke straight with me. "Steve," he said. "I can't help you, but I know someone who can. His name is Jesus. Pray with me."

"I can't," I said.

His next words were the catalyst that literally saved my life. "That's okay, Steve. Just say His name—Jesus."

In desperation I spoke His name: "Jesus." As I did, something miraculous happened. The convulsions began to cease. I cried louder, "Jesus! Jesus! Jesus!" In that instant my chains were broken, and I passed from death unto life. I was born again! I experienced firsthand that "whoever calls on the name of the LORD shall be saved" (Rom. 10:13). I was saved, healed, and delivered all at the same time, simply by calling upon the name of the Lord. That's how I came into the kingdom.

After Jeri and I were married, we were thrilled to be working for Jesus at a Teen Challenge Center. The fact that we lived on a mere seventy dollars a week between the two of us hardly fazed us. (Mind you, the poverty level back then was ninety-four dollars a week!). We were so broke that our big weekly splurge was a dollar hamburger and chocolate milkshake. But our bank account (or lack thereof) didn't affect our outlook on life. We simply trusted Jesus to take care of us and to supply our every need. We were so grateful for how Jesus saved and transformed our lives that all we wanted was to live for Him and serve Him. Nothing else mattered. Remember those days?

Today scores of young people graduate from Bible school expecting a church to give them a high-paying position with full benefits. (Where is *that* in the Bible?) And when it doesn't happen, all too often they go out and get a cushy secular job. The next thing you know, the call of God and their desire for ministry is a faint dream of the past.

Perhaps you have the call of God upon your life for ministry but have shelved it. Or maybe God once put a dream in your heart, but now it's a distant memory. My friend, it's time to remember what you used to believe.

I was reminiscing with a dear friend the other day, and we began to relive some of the exciting days of yesteryear.

Do you remember back when preachers boldly spoke about hell and we sat in those meetings shaking in our seats? Do you remember when someone would come through and talk about the Rapture? About how, at any time, Jesus would come back and we would take off like a rocket to meet Him in the air?

I remember one young evangelist talking about how Jesus worked miracles and that He would do mighty things "right now" if we would only believe. "Man, that's incredible," I said to my friend. "I've never heard of miracles for today. Let's go up there and ask Jesus for something!"

Then I remember an authoritative man telling about the baptism of the Holy Ghost. He wasn't a preacher; he was a businessman who had something awesome to say. He talked about how Jesus had to leave the earth, but He sent the Holy Ghost to fill us with power and to guide our lives. He talked about speaking in tongues and how we would receive a prayer language. "How weird," I thought.

But he showed from the Bible how speaking in tongues is for us today, and I believed. Wow! I got up from my chair, began to move toward the front, and was hit by the Spirit of God. On my way forward I began speaking in a strange new language. Later that night, while talking with friends about the Holy Ghost, I said, "This is incredible! I'm speaking in a secret language, like a private code that the devil doesn't understand." I began speaking in my prayer language that day and haven't ever stopped. Do you remember believing in that stuff?

How about testimony time? Christians would jump up like

popcorn to share their latest experience with Jesus. Do you still believe in this stuff? How many churches have allowed these life-changing experiences to drift into history? Maybe you've grown more sophisticated. Or, like many leaders, you are actually ashamed of the Holy Ghost and the evidence of tongues. You think it's embarrassing, offensive, and takes up too much time. And please don't tell me all this happens in the cell groups or life groups. I've talked to scores of Christians about this subject. It's just not happening.

Reader, please understand. I don't spend my life studying the fads and fashions of every church in town. My platter is full. I mind my own business. Jeri and I have planted powerful Pentecostal churches all over the world. There is freedom in our services to come as you are, worship out loud, speak in tongues, hear about a sweet heaven and a burning hell, grace and wrath, mercy and judgment, love, talk about the Rapture, the end of the world. We always give altar calls and still take time to pray for those who are hungry or in need.

> **Miracles happened because your head wasn't in the way. Your heart led the way.**

Our last church plant in Dallas is just like this as well. We refuse to forget where we come from as we look forward to where we are going. Pastor, it is still possible to have a relevant church in this century without abandoning what brought us through the last century.

The early days. The days of innocence. The days when you first got saved and believed God for anything. You and your friends would cast out devils and lay hands on drug addicts. Miracles happened because your head wasn't in the way. Your heart led the way.

You were a child and He was your Father. You were a King's kid! Now you're grown up and don't need Him as much. You can do it yourself. God is more like an old man, and you're like a young spiritual entrepreneur. You can figure things out for yourself and occasionally lean on Him for advice. I sense danger! I see snow.

How about the prophets who came through your church and had a word from the Lord? Sometimes you might even skip the service because this prophet or prophetess could see right through you, and that's the last thing you wanted.

And those who taught on the end of the world, the Antichrist, and the great judgments to come. They would fire me up! I was ready to take on the world with the facts of the future. Do you believe that stuff? Or is it too offensive to you and your friends now?

MORE THAN STORIES

And how about the cool stories in the Bible? Or the strange things in that Holy Book? When I truly became a believer, the Bible truly became real to me. There were no myths or fables. It was fact, from cover to cover.

The creation of man—Adam and Eve and how they were formed by God in His image and given authority over all the other living creatures. These aren't just fables for the uneducated, the simple-minded. And the Gospels are not just a history book. Here I was, and am, a grown man from an intelligent family, believing this stuff. Let me give you just a portion of my family tree.

My father was a captain in the US Army and later worked with the Army Missile Command in Huntsville, Alabama. Much of what he did was top secret. He was a brilliant man. When he came home from work, I would ask him what he did that day. "I can't tell you, Steve. It's secret. But I will say that we're planning on sending a rocket to the moon." My face lit up. That was my dad.

My mom worked on computers with the board of education. This was back when most people had never touched a computer keyboard. My older sister ran her own day care—very successfully. My older brother is also brilliant and part owner of a profitable surveying company. My younger sister is the head of a public library. She also has a room full of trophies from professionally training and riding horses. I say all this to let you know that our family has some intelligence. My mom and dad have passed away. All of us grown children are Christians, and we believe this Bible stuff.

Many are convinced Bible stories are for kids, but I'm here to say that God wasn't kidding. I want to challenge your faith. Perhaps you have moved into the intelligent stage rather than living in the innocent stage. If you can do something yourself, then it's not faith. Let me add, if you have to process everything with your brain, then it's not believing.

God created us from nothing. Your lineage is not full of worms, wooly monster-looking men, and monkeys. God created you in His image. Period!

He commanded Noah to build an ark and fill it up with animals. He flooded the earth, killed everybody, and started over. He split the Red Sea for Moses. Jonah got swallowed by a big fish and lived inside until his lesson was learned. How long do you want to stay inside that nasty place? When are you going to obey God?

Elijah called fire down from heaven. And young David killed a bully with a smooth, small, round river rock.

Jesus was born of a virgin. He raised the dead and rose from the dead. Ananias and Sapphira lied and died (in church). The disciples worked miracles, and so can you, if you believe that stuff!

John received an incredible revelation. There is a hell, and it will be filled with the devil, his demons, and all those who reject the Lord.

These aren't just stories but facts that you had better believe!

Sadly, many people used to believe all this stuff. God hasn't changed; people have. He hasn't changed His mind; you've changed yours. Scripture promises that "Jesus Christ is the same yesterday, today, and forever" (Heb. 13:8).

Do you still believe in the gifts of the Spirit, in the power of God, that tongues are for today, that Jesus is coming soon, that heaven and hell are real, that the Bible is true? Allow me to probe a little deeper.

When was the last time you spoke in tongues, laid hands on the sick, or cast out a devil? If you really believe there's a heaven to gain and a hell to shun, when was the last time you stepped out of your comfort zone and shared the gospel with someone lost and on their way to hell?

You don't want to become one of those who have a form of godliness but deny the power (2 Tim. 3:5) or who "profess to know God, but in works they deny Him" (Titus 1:16).

GETTING BACK TO THE BASICS

So what does all of this have to do with the avalanche vision the Lord gave me? Plenty! You see, those who used to believe that stuff have been affected by the snow falling upon the mountain and don't even know it.

This reminds me of a ski trip my wife and I took many years ago in the Northwest at a simple, small resort where there were no fancy gondolas, no expert ski runs, not many tourists. Most skiers were locals who had frequented the resort for at least four decades. And everybody was smiling and cheerful. Things weren't as competitive as nowadays. No fashion show. No noisy snow machines. Jeri and I had on simple, rented outfits and skis. We were enjoying the sparkling beauty of fresh, new-fallen snow and the company of simple folk.

The first ride up and down was perfect. I had conquered the mountain on my first run. A few hours into the day two young guys heading to the ski lift caught my eye. I couldn't help but notice them because of their crazy outfits. They looked so backward. They had on blue jeans rather than ski pants. They wore grandfather-type, long overcoats, and had knitted caps pulled down over their ears. They carried old wooden skis, a sight never seen even in those days. Inwardly I laughed at them. I couldn't wait to see them crash and burn trying to ski down the slopes.

This was a family-run ski hill, not a mountain, where you could watch people ride the lift all the way to the top and then see them ski to the bottom where we were located.

So Jeri and I watched the young guys get off the lift and waited for them to tumble. To our surprise they began their descent with the beauty and grace of dancing acrobats. They swooped left and right, carved the snow like Olympic gold medal winners, then spun around and skied backward, coming to a perfectly controlled stop right in front of us. I was amazed. I felt I'd just witnessed the most spectacular ski show on earth, with wooden skis and grandpappy coats, no less.

Then and there I learned a valuable lesson. You don't need all the fancy, expensive gear to go skiing—you just need to know how to ski. Those guys didn't need the latest equipment or expensive ski attire to keep them dry, because they never fell down. Now, years later, I remember how beautiful, how simple, and how fun skiing was for them, without all the modern stuff many think they need on the slopes. And so it is with our walk with Jesus.

Let's go down memory lane just a bit more. When I first got saved, I believed in miracles. I still do. I'll never forget when I was at a place called Outreach Ministries in Alabama. It was a wonderful, lifesaving haven for drug users and alcoholics. I witnessed a simple miracle that forever changed my attitude about God. I learned that He really cared about those who were down-and-out.

You see, we were out of toilet paper. It was a serious crisis. Our director, Jim Summers, gathered the residents, put us in a circle, and made us hold hands. We were instructed to ask God to provide our need. We screamed out, "God, bring us toilet paper!"

Now, how do you think God felt about a band of ex-druggies screaming for toilet paper? But then something supernatural happened. Within minutes a man, out of breath, knocked on the door and said, "I was reading my Bible, and the Lord spoke to me that there was a need for toilet paper here at your house. So I grabbed a roll and came running." Our room filled with praise for the miracle of toilet paper! What a God we serve! Do you believe stuff like that? If you do, maybe you will begin seeing stuff like that.

Would the God who created the universe perform a miracle and provide something as insignificant as toilet paper to a group of guys who cried out to Him in simple, childlike faith, and trust? Yes, indeed!

The reason people don't see miracles is because they don't *believe.* If the church would take God at His Word and step out with child-like faith, we'd see so many miracles that people would stop us in the streets and beg us to tell them about this miracle-working Man called Jesus, who said, "Whatever things you ask when you pray, believe that you receive them, and you will have them" (Mark 11:24). Isn't that simple?

Years ago as a new believer my wife was overjoyed as she heard the Word of God. Every word, every verse seemed like God was talking to her personally. Her devotion time was, and still is, the highlight of every day. From the time Jeri was saved back in 1975, she has never lived in the world of "I used to believe." She loves Jesus just as passionately today as when she gave her life to Him. She still believes in her heavenly Father with that simple, childlike faith. Nothing has changed. She still saturates herself in the Word every day, and she hasn't once stopped believing. And that's why she experiences so many miracles.

> **If the church would take God at His Word and step out with childlike faith, we'd see so many miracles that people would stop us in the streets and beg us to tell them about this miracle-working Man called Jesus.**

Perhaps you're living in the land of "I used to believe." Father God is speaking to you, calling you to return to your roots. To return to that place where "if you can believe, all things are possible to him who believes" (Mark 9:23).

REALIZING WHAT'S AT STAKE

You see, there's so much at stake, not just for you personally but also for the kingdom of God. The Lord needs those seasoned saints who've known and walked with Him over time to take the spiritual artillery He's given us and help prevent an avalanche.

He's looking for those who will set off bombs to blow up the deep piles of unbelief and false teaching. They are ruining countless lives and causing great harm to the work of God.

Today I see the beginning tremors of an enormous avalanche

under the massive snowfall of heretical and abominable teachings. With great concern pastors tell about how church members are being poisoned by the rampant error and false teaching found on Christian television and the Internet. I hurt for them because I know what it takes to pastor a flock of precious lambs. We want them drinking clean, fresh, still water and eating nutritious food for the soul.

I share comforting words with pastors and pledge to continue our efforts to destroy the avalanche before it consumes the innocent lives of our flocks. Like the ski patrol, pastors and church leaders vow to do everything possible in this battle for souls. They are committed to recruit and train people to mount an offensive attack at this demonic onslaught.

Recently while mailing some packages at a local shipping company, I took the opportunity to talk with the clerk about his soul.

I said, "Sir, what's your name?"

"Aaron," he answered.

"Aaron, my name is Steve. I want to ask you a question."

We shook hands. "Do you know Jesus Christ as your personal Savior?" He was stunned at my directness, maybe because I didn't ask if he went to church or believed in God.

Aaron looked me in the eye and without hesitation replied, "Yes, I do."

With our eyes still locked, I said, "Don't lie to me."

Then he said something that made me laugh: "If I lied to you, I would burn for eternity. So that's why I'm telling you the truth."

I grabbed Aaron's hand, shook it hard, and said, "Good for you. Someone taught you the scripture that says, 'All liars shall have their part in the lake which burns with fire and brimstone'" (Rev. 21:8).

He said, "That's right. I know Jesus Christ as my Lord and Savior, and I'm not going to hell!"

191

My friend, if you're in the place of "I used to believe," Jesus hasn't moved; you have. The Bible is as real today as when it was written. Embrace the full counsel of the Word of God, the promises and the commandments, the blessings and the curses, the truth and the mercy, the grace and the fear of the Lord, and heaven and hell. And return to the place where you believe once again.

GETTING BACK TO THE AMAZINGNESS OF GRACE

For some reason only known to the Lord, I am being reminded of a dear saint of God who would be spiritually crushed by the lack of depth in today's Christian world. Of course, I can't speak for him, but I can speak about him. He was radically saved by the grace and mercy of God. His encounter with Jesus has become known throughout the world. However, his name, his face, and his story are almost insignificant. But not to me.

> **Many have hijacked grace and stretched its benefits far past God's intentions. Just because He loves us unconditionally, doesn't mean we can stomp all over His kindness.**

Probably one of the most recognized songs in English Christianity is "Amazing Grace," published in 1779. Imagine its origin, scratched out with a quill pen on some type of crude parchment by John Newton, a slave trader who experienced the pure mercy and grace of God. Little did he know that his poetic personal prayer to Jesus would be recorded thousands of times and be adored by generations of grateful sinners who knew exactly what he was expressing. I would imagine the rendition of "Amazing

Grace" delivered by a band of bagpipes has brought overwhelming inspiration to countless millions.

Mercy is undeserved forgiveness. Grace is undeserved favor from God. We are inferior beings; He is superior. Regardless, He chooses to extend His loving-kindness toward us. He not only forgives us (mercy), but He also continues to love us (grace). Sadly, many have hijacked that grace and stretched its benefits far past God's intentions. Just because He loves us unconditionally doesn't mean we can stomp all over His kindness.

Although I don't have a quill pen and an inkwell, I've chosen to add a few modern verses to Brother Newton's beloved hymn with my mini-computer. He would be extremely offended at the following words. I believe he would be equally offended by our modern-day interpretation of this cherished characteristic of God. As you read these words, please don't take offense. My intention is to show how far we've drifted. We live in a day when many would prefer these verses over the original.

> *Amazing grace, how sweet the sound*
> *That sets me free to sin*
> *My life is fun, no price to pay*
> *It's all because of Him.*
>
> *So many sermons I have heard*
> *The altar calls were strong*
> *But thanks to grace, I fought them off*
> *It's sin where I belong.*
>
> *When I've been there ten thousand years*
> *And shared my life of ease*
> *There are martyrs here who died for Him*
> *While I lived myself to please.*

I rarely read any comments connected with my preaching or publishing. But recently I stumbled on a sad commentary.

A young man was reading about the avalanche vision on his computer. He couldn't explain why he was so overcome with emotion as he heard about the imminent disaster. He said he was deeply troubled in his spirit and felt God was telling him to make some changes in his life. He posted those feelings in a computer chat room. Many responded to his posting with opposition comments. One particularly arrogant man, apparently heartless, since the young man was now sobbing in anguish, said: "Just throw Steve Hill's avalanche vision in the trash. If those words are bothering you, just toss them, get rid of them."

The arrogant man went on to add, "Your life probably has enough troubles. It's obvious that Steve Hill's avalanche vision is producing anxiety. Throw it away." In essence he was saying, "You don't have to believe that stuff."

My friend, let's go back home. What we used to believe "then" we must believe "now." Remember, an avalanche is made up of layers upon layers of snow and ice. Let's chisel away at those layers until we find again our firm foundation.

I have been preaching, teaching, and evangelizing for decades. What I learned "back then" I preach right now. It's not fluff. You had better believe this stuff.

Whether you used to believe these things at one time and drifted away or you've never heard any of this before, the next chapter, the closing chapter of this book, is for you. Read on and discover what you can do to find your way to the truth.

Chapter 15

GET OFF the SLAB

I F YOU WERE IN SKI SCHOOL DISCUSSING THE DANGERS OF avalanches, there is one lesson that would remain in your memory forever: should you ever be picked up and carried off by an avalanche, your first job is to get off the "slab." The slab is the top layer of snow that could be carrying you down the avalanche terrain at over a hundred miles per hour. It would be up to you to find the right place and the right time to turn your skis and beat the avalanche at its game.

The same is true in a spiritual avalanche. You first need to get off the slab, get off the slide to destruction. I only want to see complete victory in every area of your life. If you've been caught up in some of the false teachings I have warned about, you need to make some serious changes right now. When you take that first step, you will slide victoriously off that slab right into the rescuing arms of your Savior.

Friend, I have poured out my heart through these pages. Many times I had to stop writing as I simply wept over the words the Father gave to me. This is more than just a book; it's a burden I carry. I understand what is at stake. I have spent my entire Christian life searching for souls destined for destruction. Through our ministry and those of our friends we have seen millions respond to the gospel and be spared from their own spiritual avalanche.

FROM MY HEART TO YOURS

In this book I've spoken so much about the condition of the church and the peril so many Christians face. Please allow me to speak directly to your heart.

Whether you know Jesus or not, there is a vicious fight taking place for your soul. You have a very real enemy who seeks to steal, kill, and destroy. Perhaps you are fully aware of the peril you face; perhaps you are not. The good news is that Jesus has come so that you might experience life in all its fullness, just as He promises: "The thief [the devil] does not come except to steal, and to kill, and to destroy. I have come that they may have life, and that they may have it more abundantly" (John 10:10).

I have one desire: to see you find that abundant life and be with Him in heaven one day. I have no doubt that you have felt the prompting of the Holy Spirit as He spoke straight to your heart. I've shared many stories with you of individuals who chose to ignore people who were trying to help them. The backcountry is littered with the lost lives of thousands of skiers whose body bags bear testimony to the dangers of not listening to good authority. And hell is filled with countless multitudes who wouldn't listen to the truth of Jesus.

There are four different types of people who are reading this book.

First, there are those who have never known the Lord. Do you know Jesus as your personal Lord and Savior? Maybe you practice a different religion, or maybe you don't believe in God at all. This is a divine appointment. God has led you to this book to let you know that He loves you and has a tremendous plan for your life.

Jesus said, "I am the way, the truth, and the life. No one comes to the Father except through Me" (John 14:6). The Bible says, "Nor is there salvation in any other, for there is no other name under heaven given among men by which we must be saved" (Acts 4:12).

A prophet cannot save you, idols will not save you, and even good works will not get you to heaven. Only genuine faith in Jesus Christ alone will save you. God sent His Son more than two thousand years ago to die for your sins. As He hung on a cruel, wooden cross, stripped of His clothing, in pain beyond description, He uttered these words that have echoed through eternity: "Father, forgive them, for they do not know what they do" (Luke 23:34). God wrapped His Son in the sins of humanity, and Jesus died for every sin you and I would ever commit.

On the third day Jesus rose from the dead. He is now in heaven wanting everyone to be with Him, because He is "not willing that any should perish but that all should come to repentance" (2 Pet. 3:9). It was through His death that we are forgiven, and it is through His resurrection from the dead that we can experience the eternal life He promised. If you've never known Jesus but would like to meet Him, we will pray together in just a moment.

Perhaps you are in the second group of readers. You're a backslider or a prodigal. You once knew the Lord but have fallen away. Sin has once again taken control of your life. It's time to come back home to the Lord. Confess your sins, and He will forgive you: "If we confess our sins, He is faithful and just to forgive us our sins and to cleanse us from all unrighteousness" (1 John 1:9). Don't wait another day.

The third type of person reading this book is the one who is religious but doesn't know the Lord. Just because you go to church doesn't mean you'll go to heaven. Walking into a garage doesn't make you a car. And walking into church doesn't make you a

Christian. Perhaps you're a church leader and have been convicted over the truth in this book. Maybe you're religious, but you've strayed. Religion is hanging around the cross, but Christianity is getting on the cross. Decide right now to get back to what you once believed. Come back to Jesus!

The fourth group of people knows the Lord and loves Him sincerely, living in victory every day. They're spiritually skiing on the right slopes. If that is you, blessings!

> **Religion is hanging around the cross, but Christianity is getting on the cross.**

If you need Jesus to cleanse you, wash away your sins, come into your heart, and be your Lord and Savior, then pray the following simple prayer. Pray it out loud! Wherever you are at this moment, why not make that spot an altar? Surrender your life to Jesus. I encourage you to get on your knees, if possible, and pray. If you're serious, He will hear you.

> *Dear Lord Jesus, thank You for speaking to me. Thank You for not leaving me alone. Thank You for Your presence in my life.*
>
> *Jesus, I have sinned. I have hurt You, hurt others, and hurt myself. I'm sorry. Forgive me; wash me; make me brand-new. Come live in my heart. Be my Savior, my Lord, and my very best Friend.*
>
> *In Your precious name, in Jesus' name, amen!*

If you just prayed this prayer, our website is full of ministry material that can answer your questions and help you grow in God. Visit us at www.stevehill.org.

Epilogue

THERE ARE OVER SEVEN BILLION PEOPLE ON PLANET EARTH. Each one of them, as they come to the age of accountability, has the innate God-given capacity to feel conviction over sin, repent to the One who can forgive them, and turn their lives around. This way of salvation was made possible by Jesus Christ, the only Son of God who was destined to die from the foundation of the world:

> ...knowing that you were not redeemed with corruptible things, like silver or gold, from your aimless conduct received by tradition from your fathers, but with the precious blood of Christ, as of a lamb without blemish and without spot. He indeed was foreordained before the foundation of the world, but was manifest in these last times for you who through Him believe in God, who raised Him from the dead and gave Him glory, so that your faith and hope are in God.
>
> —1 PETER 1:18–21

Did you see what God said? We were once "doing our own thing" aimlessly, without any sense of direction. We followed tradition, whether it was right or wrong. God knew from the beginning that we possessed a horrible sense of spiritual direction. We might know how to find our way here on earth, but without His help we would never find our way to heaven.

God's perfect, priceless plan changed all that. Through the death of Jesus *all* mankind was offered access to the holy of holies, a place of intimacy with God.

Now we have all been given a free choice. If we choose to tune our ears toward the only One worth following and listen to His instructions, we will find ourselves at the right destination. Listen; our eternal destiny is no longer determined by the laws we break but by the pain He bore on Calvary. This vision, *Spiritual Avalanche: The Threat of False Teachings That Could Destroy Millions*, was given to me while living in what we call borrowed time. I was given a few days to live, and the Lord chose to spare my life. No one knows his or her physical end. But we should all be well aware of our spiritual end.

When I received this vision, my pen hit the paper (actually my mini-computer), and I haven't stopped. You are the reason I wake up early in the morning and jump to my assignment. This book reveals the tremendous task before us and points us to our individual work assignments.

Once we've taken care of our work on earth, then we can join with the apostle Paul by saying, "I have fought the good fight, I have finished the race, I have kept the faith. Finally, there is laid up for me the crown of righteousness, which the Lord, the righteous Judge, will give to me on that Day, and not to me only but also to all who have loved His appearing" (2 Tim. 4:7–8).

Wow! Something unprecedented awaits us! Our eternal destiny excites me more than words can describe. Just as I told the waiter in chapter 8 about heaven, and he melted, I am thrilled to talk to you about eternity and the glorious life that awaits you. There is no greater way to wrap up this writing than to point everyone to our prosperous place in the kingdom to come.

This should not be a new revelation to most of us. But sadly it is a foreign subject. The more attached to this world we are, the less attracted to His world we'll be.

For my entire life prior to meeting Jesus, I gave absolutely no attention to how my life would end. Life after death was a subject that I rarely pursued. It just didn't matter until I met the Lord. From that moment on my entire focus of life changed dramatically.

Because of this change I have become known as a very intense man—a man who loves life but lives in a constant awareness that it will soon be over. These should not be gloomy words for anyone. When they are fully understood, you will say with me, "The end is far greater than the beginning." No matter how difficult or how blessed our lives have been here on earth, nothing compares to what awaits us.

I trust that we have become friends as you've read this book and that one day we will have the opportunity to connect in eternity. We are not there yet, but it is possible that we can have a taste of eternity here on earth.

As you have read several times in this book, I had the privilege of being mentored by Leonard Ravenhill. Leonard was a tremendous man of God who was more at home in the prayer closet than anywhere else. In his latter years he would spend at least six hours a day in solitude with Jesus. Imagine; he was still seeking more of the Lord in his eighties. He always had a boyish excitement when we talked about heavenly things.

Waves of enthusiasm would sweep over his soul. Listening to his bubbly British accent as he relayed a visitation he had experienced during the night caused me to crave that type of relationship with the Lord. Also, oftentimes when he got excited it meant that I would get an assignment.

Very, very early one morning Leonard called me up and said,

"Steve, I want you to make me a sign." He knew that I enjoyed graphic arts and sign painting.

While rubbing the sleep out of my eyes, I replied, "Sure, Leonard, I'd be glad to. What do you want the sign to say?"

"Eternity," was all he said.

"Eternity?"

"Yes."

"Anything else?"

"No. Just the word eternity."

"Okay." So I meticulously made the sign and brought it over to his house later that day. I've been taught to do everything for Jesus with a standard of excellence. Preparing a sign for Leonard was like preparing something for the Lord. It had to be perfect. When I asked him where he wanted the sign, he pointed up and replied, "Put it on the ceiling."

"On the ceiling?"

"Yes, right there! Now, every time I lean back in my chair and look up, I will be reminded of eternity."

Leonard lived for eternity. He was always heavenly minded. That means he lived according to this mandate from God: "Set your mind on things above, not on things on the earth" (Col. 3:2).

Brother Ravenhill went home to be with the Lord just a year after I made that sign. Now he's on the other side of eternity. He's received his reward for living passionately for God while on the earth. His epitaph reads, "Are the things you're living for, worth Christ dying for?" My wife and I have visited his grave site many times. We find ourselves thanking him for not wavering from the truth and for teaching us to keep our eyes focused on eternity.

The words you have read in this book have come from a burdened heart. I want so much for everyone to be strong in the Lord. Now, when *anything* comes against you, and I mean *anything*, you stand! As the layers of false teaching continue to fall, those who are strong will immediately sense in their spirit that something is wrong. Why? Because their spirit man overrides their carnal man. Their carnal mind is under subjection to their spiritual mind.

The apostle Paul spoke to the church at Corinth of the importance of having a firm foundation. "According to the grace of God which was given to me, as a wise master builder I have laid the foundation, and another builds on it. But let each one take heed how he builds on it. For no other foundation can anyone lay than that which is laid, which is Jesus Christ" (1 Cor. 3:10–11).

Would to God that every Christian took this scripture seriously! How it would transform our lives, not to mention our eternal reward!

I live for the day when I will stand before the Lord face-to-face. I have envisioned it for years—kneeling before Him, laying a beautiful crown at His feet, and hearing Him say, "Well done, Steve!" Anticipation of that great and glorious day has been the primary motivation of my life ever since I've known Him.

When we stand before Him, He will reward us for our works and how we lived our lives on earth:

> For the Son of Man will come in the glory of His Father with His angels, and then He will reward each according to his works.
> —MATTHEW 16:27

Heaven, my friend, keeps record of everything we do on earth.

- Every time we witnessed to someone

- Every soul that we led to Jesus

- Every time we reached out to bless someone

- Every prayer we ever prayed on behalf of others
- Every word of encouragement that was spoken
- Every dollar we sowed into the kingdom
- Every time we searched the Scriptures to test a teaching
- Every sacrifice we made for the cause of Christ
- Every act of obedience
- Every step of faith
- Everything we ever said, gave, or did to bless His name

As the years go by, you may forget many of the works that you've done in His name, but Jesus never forgets!

> For God is not unjust to forget your work and labor of love which you have shown toward His name, in that you have ministered to the saints, and do minister. And we desire that each one of you show the same diligence to the full assurance of hope until the end, that you do not become sluggish, but imitate those who through faith and patience inherit the promises.
>
> —HEBREWS 6:10–12

The Lord will not forget your work and your labor of love! He wants you to inherit His promises! That's why you must be diligent unto the end—so you can receive His reward. And most importantly, that the Son of God can receive the reward for His suffering.

We are coming to a close with this book, but in my heart I want to continue. There is so much more to be said concerning the days we are living in and the days ahead.

Without comparing myself to the apostle John, I can without

hesitation say that I was "in the Spirit" when the Lord spoke to me with the avalanche vision. Being in the Spirit means that I was not in the flesh. My mind was on the supernatural, beyond the natural. His concern over where we are now and where we are going penetrated my heart. As I stated so many times in this book, we must do something, and we must do it now. There is no more time.

The Lord will soon return with the well-deserved anticipation of gazing upon His glorious, spotless bride. He has done so much for us. In many countries the groom must pay a dowry to the father for his bride. Jesus paid the ultimate price—He gave His life! What more can we demand of Him?

I have determined it is time for us to do something special for Jesus. Like John the Baptist we must prepare the way for His return. This vision was all about cleaning up and getting ready. If we will obey this mandate in its entirety, our Lord will be presented a glorious church, without spot or wrinkle, holy and without blemish.

You do believe that He's coming back, don't you?

Then he said to me, "Write: 'Blessed are those who are called to the marriage supper of the Lamb!'" And he said to me, "These are the true sayings of God."
—REVELATION 19:9

Acknowledgments

A VERY SPECIAL NOTE OF APPRECIATION FOR THOSE WHO offered their theological knowledge, research skills, proofing, and editing expertise. I used the following scripture in the epilogue, but I must use it again here:

For God is not unjust to forget your
work and labor of love which you have
shown toward His name, in that you have
ministered to the saints, and do minister.
—Hebrews 6:10

First, I'd like to acknowledge Michael Brown, PhD, who contributed significantly to chapter 7, "Whiteout." Because of his trusted theological background, I asked him to personally vet the false teachings I was addressing in that chapter, and he graciously agreed to do so. In the process he added substantially to the truth being communicated in that segment of the book. I thank him for this invaluable service. He also invites readers who want to dialogue further about the teachings addressed in that chapter to contact him personally on his website at www.askdrbrown.org; you can also reach him at AskDrBrown on Facebook or @DrMichaelLBrown on Twitter.

Additional thanks go to the following people for lending their skills and loving support as we took this vision from God, wrote it down, and expanded it into book form: Tomi Kaiser, Kathy Duffy, Sean Duffy, Daniel Norris, Dr. Al Roever, Colorado Ski Patrol, Ronnie Rosas, Charity Merrill, Jeri Hill, Shelby Hill, Ryan Hill, Kelsey Hill, and the staff at Charisma Media.

STEVE HILL
M I N I S T R I E S

Leading the Lost to Jesus • Challenging Believers to Go After God

For over three decades this ministry has been passionately fulfilling the Great Commission. Millions are being impacted with the gospel of Jesus Christ through our worldwide crusades, television broadcasts, Internet evangelism, publications, school of evangelism, and various outreaches.

We encourage you to visit our websites for valuable resources:

STEVEHILL.ORG
contact@stevehill.org

Bringing you NEWS and VIEWS
from the FRONTLINES
of world events

PRODIGALSONLY.COM
Join the
THOUSANDS
who have come home

SERIOUS
ABOUTGOD.net
"A two-week Bible study to help you grow in God"

- Words From the World -

TURKEY *"I saw you on TV and was very impressed by the way you tell the message of Jesus. My wife and I are not Christians, but we feel closer to your way of life. Will you help us?"*

AMERICA *"I've been backslidden for years. Suicidal. I saw you on television and gave my heart to Christ. You saved my life. Thank you."*

INDIA *"I was very moved by your messages. I cannot resist crying as I feel the love of God while listening. Because of your ministry, I have given my entire life to Jesus."*

EGYPT *"I am a 26-year-old Muslim male, but now I believe in Jesus. If I declare my faith, it means death. Can one like me enter the Kingdom? Can you help me?"*

We receive thousands of responses worldwide. Many are letters of appreciation. Others are desperate cries for help. Our ministry is dedicated to changing lives. Contact us anytime.

Blessings,
Steve